W9-BYT-780

THE RESURRECTION OF JESUS
A Jewish Perspective

PINCHAS LAPIDE
Introduction by Carl E. Braaten

AUGSBURG Publishing House • Minneapolis

THE RESURRECTION OF JESUS

Library of Congress Catalog Card No. 83-70514
International Standard Book No. 0-8066-2020-X

This is a translation of *Auferstehung: Ein jüdisches Glaubenserlebnis* published in 1977 by Calwer Verlag, Stuttgart, and Kösel-Verlag GmbH & Co., München.

Manufactured in the United States of America

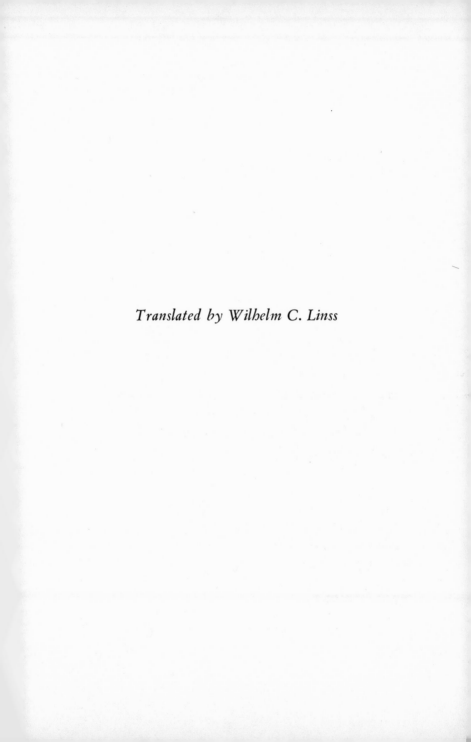

Translated by Wilhelm C. Linss

O my God, the soul which thou gavest me is pure;
thou didst create it, thou didst form it,
thou didst breathe it into me. Thou preservest
*   it within me,*
and thou wilt take it from me, but wilt restore
*   unto me hereafter.*
So long as the soul is within me, I will give
*   thanks unto thee, O Lord my God*
*   and God of my Fathers,*
Sovereign of all works, Lord of all souls!
Blessed art thou, O Lord, who restorest souls
*   unto the dead.*

Excerpt from the Morning Service (*Daily Prayer Book,* New York: Bloch, 1971, p. 19).

CONTENTS

INTRODUCTION

The Resurrection
in Jewish-Christian Dialogue

CARL E. BRAATEN

When an Orthodox Jew writes a book on the resurrection of Jesus of Nazareth, one is not surprised to see it make the "Religion" section of *Time* magazine (May 7, 1979). It is an event without precedent in the long history of Jewish-Christian relations. But when the author's main thesis favors the *historical facticity* of Jesus' resurrection, based on a critical examination of the documentary evidences, then we are witnessing some kind of ecumenical miracle. Pinchas Lapide is a leading Jewish ecumenist who has been directly engaged in a series of dialogues with many of the most eminent scholars in the world of Protestant and Catholic theology. And these dialogues deal with the most central and sensitive theological issues that divide church and synagogue. There is, for example, a Lapide-Moltmann dialogue on the Trinity,[1] one with Küng on the historical Jesus and christology,[2] with Stuhlmacher on the apostle Paul,[3] and with Pannenberg on issues that unite and separate Christianity and Judaism.[4]

Dr. Pinchas Lapide is a Jewish New Testament theologian and former associate professor at the American College in Jerusalem. During World War II he was an officer of the Jewish Brigade in the British Army, and has served the State of Israel in various roles as diplomat and head of the Jerusalem press bureau. Currently living in Frankfurt, Germany, he has been guest professor at the University of Göttingen. He continues to lecture at various European universities and publish on themes of mutual interest to Christians and Jews, leading ultimately to a more comprehensive Jewish theology of Christianity, something that has never yet been fully developed since the first century schism. Lapide's work is a challenge to Christians to respond in kind with a Christian theology of Judaism in a post-Holocaust era.

Dr. Lapide himself characterizes his approach as a process of rediscovering the authentically Jewish aspects of early Christianity, one that includes the recovery of Jesus and the witness of the first believers, who were all Jews, and even of Paul, who so far from intending to start a new religion, was perhaps the most Jewish of all Jews. Lapide calls this process *"Heimholung"* [5]—"bringing home" to Judaism today what is originally rooted in Jewish experience, thus overcoming the alienation that Jews have felt toward those elements of their own tradition which served as the foundation stones of Christianity. Thus, on account of the suffering of Jews at the hands of Christians, the very name of Jesus became tabu, and many Jews even surrendered their hope for the Messiah, as a kind of spontaneous religious protest against what Christians have made of the Messiah's coming. Christians have turned the cross into a sword and a swastika—and to this day Jews see in the cross a symbol of the Inquisition, the Crusades, the pogroms, and the Holocaust. Pinchas Lapide does not let his readers forget the painful history of Jewish agony, and yet he hopes to transcend the negativities of the past on the way to a rapprochement at a deep level of faith and theology.

A Jewish-Christian dialogue is possible today as never before. There is a "Hebrew wave" passing through Christianity in the search for roots of spiritual identity, as Jürgen Moltmann has observed, and currently from the Jewish side there is a "Jesus wave" passing through Judaism.[6] Lapide speaks of the Jewish-Christian dialogue as a conversation between the brothers and the disciples of Jesus. As evidence of a "Jesus wave" Lapide cites "the 187 Hebrew books, research articles, poems, plays, monographs, dissertations, and essays that have been written about Jesus in the last twenty-seven years since the foundation of the state of Israel." [7]

In Christian circles theologians have been involved in a kind of de-Hellenization of the gospel, overcoming the Hebraic void in the classical dogmas while rediscovering the continuing meaning of Judaism for the Christian world mission today. The age-old conflict is now being posed as a hermeneutical issue: what is the right hermeneutical key to interpret the Hebrew Scriptures? For Christians the New Testament provides the perspective for interpreting the Hebrew Bible. Professor Lapide is a Jewish New Testament theologian, and that is what is so unique about his contributions to the ecumenical dialogue. He goes to the heart of the early Christian witnesses, and finds that they all point to the history and meaning of Jesus of Nazareth, his life, teachings, cross, and resurrection.

Before Professor Lapide tackled the most controversial problem of christology, namely, the resurrection of Jesus, he had already become deeply engaged in a historical-critical reconstruction of the life and teachings of Jesus, so far as they can be known from the Gospel sources. The historical Jesus is not, purely and simply, identical with the One that any of the four evangelists portray. He is a "fifth Jesus," the Galilean rabbi whose true-to-life image is reconstructed from the sources, minus the christological overlay of believing interpretations which the post-Easter communities of faith wove into their memories of his earthly ministry. Lapide's book on "Jesus the Jew" [8] is not, of course, a product of pure scientific interest proceeding without presuppositions. To the contrary, Lapide is placing his research directly at the service of the Jewish-Christian dialogue; [9] he uses historical arguments both to break down the walls of separation and to build bridges of better mutual understanding. Where better to begin than with the very Jew whom Christians call their Lord and Savior? What better strategy than to portray Jesus of Nazareth ever a loyal son of Israel, with deep roots in the faith of his people? Jesus of Nazareth, and no one else, can serve as a bond of union between Jews and Christians, in spite of their different perspectives of faith.

Perhaps the best way to convey the intensity of Lapide's devotion to Jesus of Nazareth is to quote him directly. In his dialogue with Moltmann, and speaking in the context of a parish convocation, Lapide stated: "I accept Jesus as a believing Jew who had a central role to play in God's plan of salvation and in whose name a worldwide church was founded." [10] In his dialogue with Küng, Lapide said: "My Judaism is 'catholic' enough, in the original meaning of the word, to find a place for Spinoza as well as for Jesus, for Philo as well as for Josephus. I do not see why I should reject a person out of Judaism such as the Rabbi of Nazareth, just because some of the Christian pictures of Christ do not suit me." [11] Lapide is convinced that perhaps only a Jew with an ear to the real ground underlying the sources will discover strong affinities with the Nazarene. And with well-pointed irony he claims to feel closer to Jesus than do many Christian theologians in Europe today, some of whom still grudgingly concede the Jewishness of Jesus, perhaps still reading the Gospels through Hellenistic, if not Aryan anti-Semitic, spectacles.

For 1800 years, says Lapide, the Gentile church has

tried to de-Judaize Jesus, to Hellenize him, and to render
the name of Jesus loathsome to all Jews, for all the reasons which Rosemary R. Ruether has documented in her
book, *Faith and Fratricide*.[12] Now, just in the last years
since Auschwitz, a reverse movement has been started to
humanize Jesus, to stress the *vere homo* in the Creed of
Chalcedon, to re-Judaize and de-Hellenize the picture
of the historical Jesus, so that Jews today can reclaim
him as their blood brother, a fellow Jew, an Israelite by
birth and birthplace, by language and religion, and by
love for his people and his people's God.

The result of Lapide's re-Judaizing of Jesus is to de-
bunk some common misconceptions that die hard in the
popular tradition. One is that the people of Israel rejected Jesus, and another is that Jesus rejected his people.
Nothing could be further from the truth. In fact, the
mother church in Jerusalem, the earliest believers, and
all the original apostles were Jews, and "multitudes" in
his day gave him an enthusiastic reception; never once
did any imagine that their belief in Jesus constituted a
break with the Hebrew faith. Nor did Jesus reject his
people. As Lapide examines the evidence, he points out
that the harshest words of Jesus against the "scribes and
pharisees" indicate only that he had opponents among
some of the leaders at that time. That Jesus stood in conflict and contrast with his age places him in the great line
of Jewish prophets, and rather than it being a sign of his
un-Jewishness or rejection of Israel, it stands as the most
telling proof of his greatness. Moses was in constant

conflict with his own people, and yet there has never been a greater Jew than he.

Hasn't Lapide overdrawn the picture of Jesus' continuity with the Jewish tradition? Why then was Jesus liquidated, Küng asks, if it was not because he challenged the Law and its authority? [13] Here too Lapide will not give any ground. By all the reports of Jesus' actions, he never broke a single commandment; he was neither a blasphemer nor a lawbreaker. "This Jesus was utterly true to the Torah, as I myself hope to be. I even suspect that Jesus was more true to the Torah than I, an orthodox Jew." [14] Yet, there comes a point of the parting of the way between Jews and Christians, and that also must be explained historically. Just where does that point lie in Lapide's view?

Lapide boldly asserts that "Jews and Christians can walk together until Good Friday" and he believes they "can remain together until Easter Monday and even conceive of the resurrection in Jewish terms," [15] but what Jews cannot accept is the messiahship of Jesus, the belief that he is the "eschatological watershed," the bringer of the kingdom of God which Jews have longed and prayed for from earliest times until now. What really separates Jews from Christians, according to Lapide, is not the 33 years of Jesus' life and ministry, a career in the service of God for which Jews today have every reason to be proud, but it is the contradictory interpretation placed on the final 48 hours from Good Friday to Easter Sunday, the decisive events—cross and resurrection—on which the whole of Christianity is based.[16] For Christians these events reveal the messianic identity of Jesus; for Jews who are still looking for the Messiah to establish the kingdom, these events do not convincingly prove the messiahship of Jesus, for when the Messiah brings in the kingdom, the world will be utterly changed in a dramatic way. But the world has not changed, not as long as there is genocide, racism, violence, war, nuclear insanity, poverty, hunger, and the like. For when the Messiah comes, the reign of God is established—an era of peace, righteousness, and fulfillment for all. Jews are still waiting for the coming of the Messiah and the dawn of such a new age. Christians also, realistically facing a world mired in sin and evil, must look forward to the future advent of the Messiah who will set things right once and for all.

Lapide puts the difference between Christianity and Judaism this way. "Christianity is a who-religion, Judaism a what-religion. Or, if you will, Judaism is a religion of redemption; Christianity one with a redeemer. For you Christians what is important is the redeemer, the king; for us it is the kingdom. We Jews know—under God—of a kingdom of heaven also, without a Savior-King; but we do not know a Savior-King with the kingdom already having come. Every morning television and the press confirm with terrible clarity that this world is not yet redeemed." [17]

Both Judaism and Christianity are messianic religions; they differ in how they perceive this messianism. Christians put Jesus the Messiah in the center, but Jews put the kingdom which the Messiah brings. Which side is right? Who was Jesus of Nazareth? Was he the Messiah? Has the kingdom come already? What kinds of evidence do we have to support our respective claims? The dialogue between Christians and Jews is now probing the deep dimensions of such sensitive theological questions as these, rather than floating around in nebulous generalities. And renewed preoccupation with the accounts of witnesses to the resurrected Jesus—by Lapide's count 530 such witnesses, all of them Jews—is just such an example that the dialogue has come of age theologically speaking.

Lapide's approach is unique among Jewish participants in the dialogue in that he accepts the resurrection of Jesus as a historical event which triggered that messianic apostolic movement whose members soon came to be called "Christians," though still all good believing Jews. In Lapide's own words: "I accept the resurrection of Easter Sunday not as an invention of the community of disciples, but as a historical event." [18] And the details of his argument are now set forth in this book, *The Resurrection of Jesus: A Jewish Perspective*. Lapide explains his thesis of the historicity of the resurrection in these words: "I am completely convinced that the Twelve from Galilee, who were all farmers, shepherds, and fishermen—there was not a single theology professor to be found among them—were totally unimpressed by scholarly theologoumena, as Karl Rahner or Rudolf Bultmann write them. If they, through such a concrete historical event as the crucifixion, were so totally in despair and crushed, as all the four evengelists report to us, then no less concrete a historical event was needed in order to bring them out of the deep valley of their despair and within a short time to transform them into a community of salvation rejoicing to the high heavens." [19]

Professor Lapide is very much aware that some of the mainline schools of theology have relegated the resurrection to the category of myth or legend or hallucination without any real basis in historical fact, and that he, although a Jew and fully at home in the use of the critical-historical method, is bringing his support to the conservative side in the debate. In fact, there is very little I can see that Wolfhart Pannenberg or Ulrich Wilckens could not accept in Lapide's argument, except that for Lapide the decision for the resurrection is finally a matter of faith, whereas Pannenberg attempts to base the assent to the resurrection on historical reason. But they reach the same conclusion: the resurrection of Jesus was a real historical occurrence, and not something first and foremost taking place in the hearts and minds of the first believers. The crucifixion of Jesus by itself could not have motivated the courage of martyrdom and unquenchable hope for the cause of salvation which Jesus preached and embodied in his actions. Jesus' resurrection convinced his disciples that he would return soon as the Messiah of Israel, and in the power of this Easter hope they carried the gospel to the nations, aiming to convert them to the worship of the One God of Israel, Father of Abraham, Isaac, and Jacob. But for the resurrection of Jesus Christianity would never have left the environs of Jerusalem, and, as Lapide put it in response to a questioner, "You, my dear friend, would today still be offering horsemeat to Wotan on the Godesberg." [20] And some of us would still be worshiping Thor, the god of thunder, whose magic hammer made loud noises in the heavens, something etched in my consciousness by the fact my father's name was Torstein.

If Lapide believes in the resurrection of Jesus, why is he then not a Christian? What stands in the way of baptism? Lapide's answer is very simple: Because the resurrection does not prove that Jesus is the Messiah, whereas to be a Christian is to believe just that. Yes, the resurrection of Jesus really happened, but no, this doesn't prove he is the Messiah. This sounds strangely paradoxical to Christians. It is precisely the aim of the book to explain this paradox. When the resurrection of Jesus is viewed from the standpoint of Jewish faith, there is no necessary link to the claim of messiahship. What then does the resurrection mean, if not God's ratification of the messianic identity and vocation of Jesus? It means, for Lapide, that Jesus belongs to the *praeparatio messianica*— the line of the great patriarchs and prophets of Israel —pioneering the full salvation of the future kingdom which God will establish through the Messiah in the last days.

If Jesus' resurrection is evidence of his preparatory

role in messianic history, why did only a small minority
of Jews come to believe in him as the linchpin of the
ongoing history of salvation which God was broadening
to include all the nations, and not only Israel? The answer is that if the majority of Jews had not said no
to the apostolic message about Jesus, Christianity would
have remained an intra-Jewish affair. It took a minority
of Jews to say yes to Jesus and a majority to say no
to drive the history of salvation beyond the particular-
ism of Judaism to the universal horizon of all nations
by way of the Gentile mission. According to the "pedagogy of God" the pagan nations could become heirs of
Jewish monotheism only on the condition of the Jewish
refusal of the gospel.

Such a contemporary Jewish theology of Christianity's validity owes a great deal to the creative thinking
of Franz Rosenzweig, whom Lapide frequently quotes.
Rosenzweig was an agnostic humanist Jew who met
Eugen Rosenstock-Huessy, a convinced Christian philosopher of religion, one day at Leipzig University in
1913. That began a series of discussions that led to a crisis
in Rosenzweig's life, at first placing him on the brink of
Christian baptism, but finally driving him back home
to Judaism. Thereafter Rosenzweig and Rosenstock
carried on a brisk correspondence,[21] converted Jew and
convinced Christian, confronting each other in an existential dialogue unparalleled in the history of Jewish-
Christian relations. In this exchange of views with his
Christian friend, Rosenzweig developed his final insight

into the compatibility of Judaism and Christianity in God's universal plan of salvation. Basically his view holds that Christianity is the Judaizing of the pagans. The task of Christianity is to preach the gospel among the Gentiles. What began with Judaism must finally end with the nations, and Christians are the go-between. The Christianizing of the nations means indirectly the triumph of Judaism in its innermost meaning and aim. The task of Judaism meanwhile is to remind Christianity of its original biblical roots, otherwise Christianity will ultimately be assimilated into paganism. The vocation of Judaism is to remain separate, while Christianity is to go forward "conquering" the world, always running the risk of being absorbed into its worldly setting. Rosenzweig's book, *The Star of Redemption*,[22] represents an outpouring of his mature philosophy of life, including his ideas about Christianity and Judaism.

Following in the tradition of Rosenzweig, Lapide sees "that the coming-to-believe of Christendom was without doubt a God-willed messianic act, a messianic event on the way to the conversion of the world to the One God." [23] All human beings are "anonymous monotheists," longing for the message which first dawned in Jewish consciousness and which the Christian mission is spreading around the world in its distinctive trinitarian form. Even if Jews cannot accept the church's doctrine of the Trinity, because they cannot accept the arrival of the Messiah in Jesus as an eschatological event, nevertheless they do acknowledge that Christianity is a trinitarian monotheism, and that Christians are, despite all, "odd monotheists," and not tritheists after all.

Rosenzweig and Lapide thus teach that Judaism and Christianity are two roads that lead to the Father. When Jesus said, "No one comes to the Father, but by me" (John 14:6), he meant no one except those who are already with the Father, and they are the Jews. Jews do not need Christ to come to the Father, since their knowledge of the Father goes back to Abraham and Moses. But Christ brings the knowledge of the Father into the world of the Gentiles, and thus the Christian church functions as an institution of salvation alongside of Israel for the sake of all the nations. To ask Jews then to convert to Christianity would be "to sprinkle sugar on top of honey," [24] for Jews are already in a sense at the goal to which the church is leading the nations. Thus, Christianity has salvation-historical meaning, if not for Jews, then for the wider Gentile world. Through his death and resurrection Christ has become the Savior of the Gentiles. To Jews who still look for the coming of the Messiah, Jesus of Nazareth can be a sign of hope along the way, renewing faith in the future fulfillment of the promises of God. Meanwhile, Jews do not know now who the coming Messiah will be. Christians claim to know that he is none other than Jesus of Nazareth, whose identity will be openly revealed to all in the end, when every tongue will "confess that Jesus Christ is Lord, to the glory of God the Father" (Phil. 2:11). And if the coming Messiah in that day should reveal himself to be identical with the one whom Christians confess has already come as Jesus of Nazareth, then Lapide graciously avows: "I cannot imagine that even a single Jew who believes in God would have the least thing against that . . . Should the coming one be Jesus, he would be precisely as welcome to us as any other whom God would designate as the redeemer of the world. If he would only come!" [25]

Meanwhile, until the eschatological coming of the Messiah—for Jews his first and only coming, for Christians his second and final coming—the "who-what debate" between Christians and Jews will continue, and no one side will coalesce into the other. Jews will go on praying *for* the Messiah, not knowing his name, and Christians will continue to pray *to* the Messiah, confessing "no other name" than Jesus Christ the Nazarene through whom God is working out his universal plan of salvation. Both sides in the debate have a *continuing* meaning in the world-historical scheme of things, according to Paul in Romans 9–11. Judaism will always be a reminder to Christians that the kingdom (the "what") is yet to come; Christians will stress that the king (the "who") has already arrived. In the end the king and the kingdom will be fully and perfectly revealed indivisibly as one; meanwhile both Christians and Jews experience the agony of their empirical separation. It is not enough, not even for Christians, that the king has come; the kingdom itself must come! It is not enough that the Redeemer has come; the redemption itself in its eschatological fullness must come! It is not enough that the Prince of Peace is with us; peace itself, not only the absence of war, but shalom in its fullest sense, must reign throughout the cosmos. Until that happens the prophecies are like prescriptions that have not yet been filled.

Christian theology is being stimulated to respond to the challenge of Jewish thinkers like Franz Rosenzweig, Martin Buber, Abraham Heschel, David Flusser, Pinchas Lapide, and many others. As they confront us with a Jewish theology of Christianity, with what Christian theology of Judaism do we respond? Some responses from the Christian side have already emerged. Church bodies have become officially involved. Roman Catholics have followed the official guidelines of Vatican II,[26] and the pope in 1974 instituted a commission for religious relations with Judaism, joined to the Secretariat for Promoting Christian Unity. The World Council of Churches has held consultations [27] on "The Church and the Jewish People," and both the Lutheran World Federation [28] and the Lutheran Council in the USA [29] have been involved in official dialogues and issued statements that bear on many facets of the relations between Christians and Jews. Individual theologians have forged new directions in theology under the impact of the Holocaust, in an attempt to root out the last vestiges of Christian anti-Judaism.[30]

It is impossible in this introduction to summarize and evaluate all that has been accomplished. Yet, there is one disturbing trend in the newer Christian approach to

Jews that warrants a serious theological warning signal. That is the tendency to compensate for millennia of Christian anti-Semitism, stirred by feelings of guilt for Christian complicity in the Nazi Holocaust, by a kind of overreaction that relativizes the gospel down to one of many ways of salvation, that surrenders the exclusive place of Christ in doing "theology after Auschwitz," and that lays the blame of hatred of the Jews on a so-called theological anti-Semitism. The charge of theological anti-Semitism can be a reckless blow directed not only at the high christology of the church fathers but also at the apostolic core of the New Testament kerygma! Rosemary R. Ruether's book, *Faith and Fratricide*, however so laudable in its goal of getting rid of the theological roots of anti-Semitism, is an example of throwing out the christological baby with the anti-Judaic bath in Christian tradition. She does so under her formula, "Anti-Judaism is the Left Hand of Christology." In other words, the heart of New Testament christology under her diagnosis is diseased; but the operation she administers leaves the patient mortally wounded. Rosemary Ruether asks whether it is really "possible to say 'Jesus is Messiah' without, implicitly or explicitly, saying at the same time, 'and the Jews be damned'?" [31] The answer Ruether proposes lifts the condemnation of Jews at the expense of the primitive apostolic witness to the pivotal place of Jesus of Nazareth in the eschatological salvation of the world, for such a place, she believes, is the breeding ground of traditional Christian anti-

Judaism. I seriously doubt that such a strategy will work: rooting out Christian contempt for Jews by lowering the messianic profile of Jesus, thus, in effect, assigning to the Christ-event a pre-eschatological significance. Christian faith in Jesus as the Christ is not the cause of prejudice, nor will a low ebionitic christology in exchange for the high christology of the church administer a cure.

An authentic Christian theology of Israel will necessarily work with the fundamental axioms of the New Testament documents on which Christianity is based. In closing this introduction we will attempt to highlight those that seem most essential.

The first principle of crucial significance is that the Hebrew Scriptures are part of the biblical canon. Early Christianity fought victoriously to retain the Old Testament against the heresy of Marcion, and the same battle had to be waged once again against the Aryan heresy of the "German Christians" under the Nazis. For Jesus and the early church the Old Testament was their only Bible, and the God whom it reveals as the Father of Abraham, Isaac, and Jacob is identical with the Father whose Son is Jesus of Nazareth. The authors of the New Testament make their case for Christian faith with arguments advanced "according to the Scriptures," meaning the Old Testament.

The second principle is that Israel continues to be the chosen people of God *post-Christum* and to have meaning in the salvation-historical scheme of things. There is a triumphalist version of Christendom which has argued that when Christ came, he liquidated the meaning of Israel, and put the church in its place. This supersessionist theory means that Israel no longer has any theological significance as the "people of God" for the church. Judaism is handled as just one of the other world religions, and not a special aspect of the church's ecumenical problem. Karl Barth, I think, was right when he said: "The Jews are without any doubt at all the chosen people of God down to this day, in the same sense as they were from the beginning according to the Old and New Testaments. They have God's promise, and if we Christians from among the Gentiles also have this promise, then we have it as those chosen along with them, as guests come into their house, as branches grafted on to their trees." [32]

The third principle holds that in the end "all Israel will be saved." (Rom. 11:26). This means that not only those Jews who are now individually converted to the gospel one by one will be saved in the end, namely, the Jewish Christians, but in the context of the parousia there will be a mass conversion of Israel to the Messiah of God. This means that God has not written off his people, but Israel will be part of the final restitution of all things (the *apokatastasis*), and God will deal with Israel as with all others on the basis of his mercy.

The fourth principle is that "salvation is from the Jews," (John 4:22). This means that God's promises are mediated to universal history through the particular history of Israel. As Paul says in Romans 9:4-5: "They are Israelites, and to them belong the sonship, the glory, the covenants, the giving of the law, the worship, and the promises; to them belong the patriarchs, and of their race, according to the flesh, is the Christ." From the history of Israel's election as a special people, the world has received its prophetic insistence on monotheism, the hope for universal salvation, a messianic and eschatological interpretation of history, the doctrine of the world as creation and utterly other than the Creator, and finally the name of Jesus the Jew as the incarnation of the Son of God.

The fifth principle is that the fact of Israel reminds the eschatological community of Christ that it lives "between the times," between the "already now" and the "not yet" of the history leading from promise to fulfillment. History is not yet the match for the hopes of Israel. There is an overdose of hope in the history of promise that drives both Israel and the church to be moving forward restlessly with an incurable case of "messianitis." Jewish rabbis of old never tired of saying, "If it is true that the Messiah of which our ancient prophets spoke has already come, how then do you explain the present state of the world?" [33]

There is actually no specific limit to the principles we could adduce in a prospective Christian theology of Judaism. But perhaps one final point should be added. As some Christian theologians debated the "the death of God" two decades ago, and as "natural theology" still today is attempting to establish the meaning of "God" in a secular age, Jewish theologians can remind us that these approaches are posing the problem of God in a very un-biblical and un-Jewish manner. They put the question of God in a very abstract manner, apart from what he has done in the *events* of history. They are dealing with the death of the gods of their own speculation, mere "scarecrows in a cucumber field" (Jer. 10:5), whose demise makes no difference to what is happening in the real world.

Paul van Buren, one of the so-called death of God theologians of the sixties, wrote the obituary of God in his book, *The Secular Meaning of the Gospel*. His latest book, *Discerning the Way*, is a sketch of a theology of the Jewish Christian reality and represents a 180-degree reversal of position, wherein he recants the secular nonsense he wrote about God in his earlier treatise. In his latest book he speaks of God, not in some newly discovered secular sense, but in a biblical sense. "The Bible," he says, "recalls to us the God who has ever dealt with His creatures in historical, temporal fashion, not as an Absolute outside of history and time." [34] It seems that Paul van Buren recovered his confidence in the meaning of God when he turned from the philosophy of logical positivism to the history of Israel's suffering and survival. Franz Rosenzweig tells of a pastor who was asked for the proof of Christianity by Frederick the Great, and he answered conclusively, "Your majesty, the Jews!" [35] Even under the present ambiguous conditions of history, there remains a mysterious depth in that response.

NOTES

1. *Jewish Monotheism and Christian Trinitarian Doctrine,* a Dialogue by Pinchas Lapide & Jürgen Moltmann, trans. by Leonard Swidler (Philadelphia: Fortress Press, 1981).
2. Hans Küng & Pinchas Lapide, *Jesus im Widerstreit, Ein jüdisch-christlicher Dialog* (Stuttgart: Calwer Verlag, 1976).
3. Pinchas Lapide & Peter Stuhlmacher, *Paulus — Rabbi und Apostel, Ein jüdisch-christlicher Dialog* (Stuttgart: Calwer Verlag, 1981).
4. Pinchas Lapide & Wolfhart Pannenberg, *Judentum und Christentum-Einheit und Unterschied* (München: Chr. Kaiser Verlag, 1982).
5. Pinchas Lapide, *Israelis, Jews, and Jesus,* trans. by Peter Heinegg (Garden City, N.Y.: Doubleday & Co., 1979), p. 81.
6. Pinchas Lapide & Ulrich Luz, *Der Jude Jesus, Thesen eines Juden, Antworten eines Christen* (Zürich, Benziger Verlag, 1979), p. 15.
7. *Israelis, Jews, and Jesus,* pp. 31-32.
8. *Der Jude Jesus.*
9. *Israelis, Jews, and Jesus,* p. 33.
10. *Jewish Monotheism and Christian Trinitarian Doctrine,* p. 76.
11. *Jesus im Widerstreit,* p. 7.
12. Rosemary Radford Ruether, *Faith and Fratricide: The Theological Roots of Anti-Semitism* (New York: The Seabury Press, 1974).
13. *Jesus im Widerstreit,* p. 35.
14. *Ibid.,* p. 26.
15. *Jewish Monotheism and Christian Trinitarian Doctrine,* p. 67.
16. *Jesus im Widerstreit,* p. 21.
17. *Ibid.,* p. 43.
18. *Jewish Monotheism and Christian Trinitarian Doctrine,* p. 59.
19. *Ibid.,* p. 60.
20. *Ibid.,* p. 68.
21. *Judaism Despite Christianity, The "Letters on Christianity and Judaism" between Eugen Rosenstock-Huessy and Franz Rosenzweig,* edited by Eugen Rosenstock-Huessy (University of Alabama Press, 1969).
22. Franz Rosenzweig, *The Star of Redemption,* trans. from the Second Edition of 1930 by William W. Hallo (New York: Holt, Rinehart and Winston, 1970).
23. *Jewish Monotheism and Christian Trinitarian Doctrine,* p. 71.
24. *Ibid.,* p. 70.
25. *Ibid.,* p. 79.

26. See John M. Oesterreicher, *The Rediscovery of Judaism: A Re-examination of the Conciliar Statement on the Jews* (South Orange, N.J.: Institute of Judaeo-Christian Studies, Seton Hall University, 1971).
27. *Faith and Order Paper #50: The Church and the Jewish People,* 1967 (Geneva: World Council of Churches, 1968).
28. *Lutheran World.* Vol. 10: "The Church and the Jews" (October, 1963). *Lutheran World.* Vol. 11: "Christians, Jews and the Mission of the Church" (July 1964).
29. Paul D. Opsahl and Marc C. Tanenbaum, *Speaking of God Today: Jews and Lutherans in Dialogue* (Philadelphia: Fortress Press, 1974).
30. For example, Gregory Baum, *Is the New Testament Anti-Semitic? A Re-Examination of the New Testament* (New York: Paulist Press, 1965).
   Alan T. Davies, *Anti-Semitism and the Christian Mind: The Crisis of Conscience after Auschwitz* (New York: Herder & Herder, 1969).
   A. Roy Eckardt, *Elder and Younger Brothers: The Encounter of Jews and Christians* (New York: Charles Scribner's Sons, 1967).
   Rosemary Radford Ruether, *Faith and Fratricide: The Theological Roots of Anti-Semitism* (New York: The Seabury Press, 1974).
   Eva Marie Fleischner, *Judaism in German Christian Theology Since 1945: Christianity and Israel Considered In Terms of Mission* (Metuchen, N.J.: The Scarecrow Press, 1975).
   Paul M. van Buren, *Discerning the Way: A Theology of the Jewish Christian Reality* (New York: The Seabury Press, 1980).
31. *Faith and Fratricide,* p. 246.
32. Quoted by Eva Marie Fleischner, *Judaism in German Christian Theology Since 1945,* p. 121.
33. *Israelis, Jews and Jesus,* p. 84.
34. Paul van Buren, *Discerning the Way,* p. 150.
35. *The Star of Redemption,* p. 415.

PROLOGUE

When one asks the basic question of what separates
Jews and Christians from each other, the unavoidable
answer is: a Jew.

For almost two millennia, a pious, devoted Jew has
stood between us, a Jew who wanted to bring the kingdom of heaven in harmony, concord, and peace—certainly not hatred, schism, let alone bloodshed.

Perhaps the most Jewish characteristic of the Nazarene is his immortal, powerful hope which found its
pinnacle, beyond cross and tomb, in the faith in his
resurrection—a faith which, in the unsearchable ways of
God for salvation, led to the birth of Christianity.

In the process of the parting of our ways of faith,
this resurrection has become a stumbling block between
the brothers of Jesus and his disciples, but, as with many

of our separations, it can be defused if it is traced back to its origins.

For that which happened on the "third day" in Jerusalem is in the last analysis an experience of God which enters into the realm of things which cannot be proved, just as God himself is unprovable; it can be grasped only by faith.

A faith which is lived can be neither refuted nor confirmed; it can only be sensed with empathy because "Our God is a God of salvation; and to God, the Lord, belongs escape from death" (Ps. 68:20).

"But If Christ Has Not Been Raised . . ."

Christianity as a historical religion of revelation is based on two fundamental events—the death of Jesus of Nazareth on the cross and his resurrection. While the first event may be considered historically certain, both according to statements of the evangelists which are basically in agreement, and also from non-Christian sources, the latter event is still controversial, cannot be conceived historically, and has led from the beginning to doubt, discord, and dissension.

In the passion narrative, all Gospels, despite many differences in details, follow a single main strand of tradition. In contrast, with regard to the Easter narratives, one cannot even speak of a literary skeleton which they have in common. In addition, there is the fact that the crucifixion of Jesus finds an echo both in rabbinic literature and in Roman-Greek writings. But the New Testament remains the only source for the resurrection which is not mentioned anywhere else outside of the canon of the church. Resurrection, exaltation, and glorification are understood not as Jesus' own deed, but, in good Jewish manner, as a raising by God, as a gracious deed of God on the crucified Jesus.

Resurrection is by far the more important of these two pillars of the Christian faith. The crucifixion was basically only its necessary precondition which later, seen in retrospect after Easter, could be transfigured and reinterpreted as significant for the history of salvation. Without the experience of the resurrection, the crucifixion of Jesus would most likely have remained without consequences and forgotten, just as were the innumerable crucifixions of pious Jews which the Romans carried out before Jesus, during the lifetime of Jesus, and up until the destruction of Jerusalem in the year 70.

In the words of Flavius Josephus, an eyewitness, which remind the reader vividly of Golgotha:

> when they (Jewish fugitives) were . . . taken, . . . they were first whipped, and then tormented with all sorts of tortures before they died, and were then crucified before the wall of the city. . . . He (Titus) hoped the Jews might, perhaps, yield at that sight, out of fear lest they might themselves afterward be liable to the same cruel treatment. So the soldiers, out of the wrath and hatred they bore the Jews, nailed those they caught, one after one way, and another after an-

other, to the crosses, by way of jest; when their
multitude was so great that room was wanting
for the crosses, and crosses wanting for the bodies
... (*Wars of the Jews,* Book V, XI, 1-2).

Thus the Christian faith stands and falls not with
Golgotha, the infamous "place of a skull," where thousands of Jesus' brothers were murdered cruelly by Roman mercenaries, but with the experience "on the third
day" after the crucifixion, an experience which was able
to defuse, to refute, and even to make meaningful this
death on the cross for the community of the disciples.
"If Christ has not been raised," Paul writes to the Corinthians, "then our preaching is in vain and your faith is
in vain" (1 Cor. 15:14).

This unequivocal confession proves not only how early
the faith in the resurrection of the Nazarene became the
cornerstone of Christianity and how central and indispensable the Easter event is and remains for the church,
but also the drastic character of the Pauline alternative.

For almost 2,000 years, popes, bishops, and church
councils as well as pragmatists—at first unbaptized,
lately also baptized—have taken the apostle to the Gentiles at his word. During the first centuries of the Christian era, this Easter confidence remained the faith of a
small number of people while the overwhelming majority, both of Jews and Gentiles, acted toward it with skepticism, often sarcastically, at times also with biting irony.

No wonder, for in no other area of the New Testament narrative are the contradictions so glaring. No-

where else are the opposites so obvious and the contrast-
ing descriptions so questionable as in the realm of the
resurrection of Jesus. Eduard Schweizer states with
regret,

> As soon as we seek to penetrate more closely and
> find out details, our sources fail us. . . .
>
> We must first of all recognize that the Gospels
> themselves exhibit no more knowledge than this
> of the resurrection, except for the appearance of
> Jesus to the eleven disciples. According to Luke
> 24:34, to be sure, the disciples in Jerusalem still
> speak of an appearance to Peter; but this very
> passage shows that only a formula was known. . . .
> Nothing more could be said. Even weightier is
> the evidence of Matthew, according to whom
> the appearance took place in Galilee. This must
> have been the first appearance, since the disciples
> still doubted; it was clearly also the only appear-
> ance, since no other is mentioned. . . . According
> to Luke, however, this appearance took place in
> Jerusalem on Easter Sunday, and the disciples
> were expressly forbidden to leave the city before
> Pentecost. The same holds true in John's account,
> albeit Jesus' appearance is described in quite dif-
> ferent terms, with a repetition a week later in
> Jerusalem and later still in Galilee. But there are
> still more difficulties. Paul clearly thinks all the
> appearances were . . . appearances from heaven.
> . . . Matthew himself probably pictures the scene

as taking place on earth, for he has added, "Jesus
came and said to them." It is clear, however, that
this is Matthew's own interpolation into the tradition he received. . . . According to Luke, however, the risen Lord walked upon the earth with
"flesh and bones," and ate with his disciples.
(*Jesus*, tr. by David E. Green, Richmond: John
Knox, 1976, pp. 46f.).

Joachim Jeremias concludes in regard to the Easter
narratives of the Gospels, "the picture is quite a varied
one" and explains:

This is true, first, of the *people involved*. The
Risen One appears now to an individual, now to
a couple of disciples, now to a small group, now
to an enormous crowd. The witnesses are mostly
men, but also women; they are members of the
inmost group of disciples, . . . but also sceptics
. . . in at least one instance we have a fanatical
opponent. . . . The variety of *locations* is as great
as the variety of witnesses: now the Christophany
takes place in the open air, now in a house, repeatedly before the gates of the holy city, then
again within Jerusalem, in a Judean village, on
the shore of Lake Gennesaret, in the hill-country
of Galilee, one even outside Palestine (*New Testament Theology: The Proclamation of Jesus*, tr.
John Bowden, New York: Scribner's, 1971, p.
330f.).

Hans Küng writes under the title "Legends?":

The history of the resurrection tradition reveals
problematical *expansions, elaborations* and occa-
sionally even gaps. The *oldest Easter testimony* of
the New Testament—the ancient formula of
faith in the first epistle to the Corinthians, already mentioned—like other Pauline formulas of
faith, has the brevity of recorded minutes, a
minimum of information without any sort of description and without any indication of the place
and time of the appearances. Even the oldest
Easter account in the Gospels . . . is amazingly
jejune. This account in *Mark* . . . adds nothing
new apart from the tradition of the empty tomb
and the reference to Jesus' appearance in Galilee.
. . . In *Matthew* . . . there are several new features: the earthquake; the story of the guards
at the tomb and the carrying out of the order of
the angel and Jesus to go to Galilee; the appearance to the eleven on the mountain in Galilee. . . .
In *Luke,* who simply omits the order to go to
Galilee, passes over the Galilean appearance and
concentrates the whole Easter event in place and
time on Jerusalem which for him is theologically
and ecclesially important, there are other additions: the artistically elaborated narrative about
the Emmaus disciples; the appearance to the eleven in Jerusalem; a brief farewell discourse and
a short account of an ascension of Jesus. . . . The
considerably later Gospel of John . . . likewise

> contains new elements and motifs: the conversation with Mary Magdalene, the wager of Peter and the unnamed beloved disciple, the gathering in the room in Jerusalem with the gift of the Spirit in the evening of Easter day, the story of the unbelieving Thomas. . . . Later a further chapter was added, . . . with the appearance on the lake of Gennesaret, a miraculous draught of fishes with a meal and a special mandate to Peter (*On Being a Christian*, Garden City: Doubleday, 1976, p. 351f.).

The empty tomb of which Paul, the earliest Christian author, does not yet have knowledge, is typical of these incongruencies. In order to avoid the accusation of fraud, Matthew tells of a guard at the tomb, a circumstance which is unfamiliar to Mark. In Mark, the women meet an angel who sits quietly in the empty tomb. In Matthew, however, the angel comes down from heaven which causes the guards (who are missing in Mark) to fall down as dead. In Mark, three women come to the tomb, in Matthew only two. They meet the angel in front of the tomb while in Mark they encounter the angel inside the tomb.

Even if the narrative of the empty tomb should have a historical kernel, it made faith in the resurrection even more difficult for some people. For a tomb which is so empty that doubt can nest in it had to give cause to sinister misinterpretations, as, e.g., fraud by the disciples, grave robbery, confusion, or trance, as the evangelists already report and as numerous authors since have attempted to reconstruct the events with irony or dry facticity.

The inclination to "secondary elaboration," as Joachim Jeremias calls it, can even be demonstrated quantitatively: While Paul, who was closest to the events, needs only four sentences (1 Cor. 15:3-7) to express his faith in the resurrection, Mark, decades later, needs eight. After him, Matthew expands the report to 20 verses, followed by Luke who is able to report later more than twice this amount—53 verses. The Fourth Gospel, edited two generations after Easter, long after the last eyewitnesses were deceased, devotes two full chapters of altogether 56 verses to the theme, in order to describe what its author could know only by hearsay.

The later a report, the more is to be narrated; the further the distance from the event itself, the more colorful is the description.

Doubt and unbelief toward the messenger of the resurrection are as old as the message itself. Among the apostles were some who were unable to believe in Jesus' resurrection, as Matthew testifies explicitly, even after the appearance of the risen Jesus in Galilee, "but some doubted" (Matt. 28:17). Already in Mark (16:14) we read, "Afterward he appeared to the eleven themselves as they sat at table; and he upbraided them for their unbelief . . . because they had not believed those who saw him after he had risen."

Luke says of the whole group of apostles who had just

heard the report of the women about the empty tomb
(24:11), "But these words seemed to them an idle tale,
and they did not believe them."

Even after the Risen One had showed himself to them
and had demonstrated his physical identity, it says of the
disciples that "they still disbelieved" (Luke 24:41). Af-
terwards, the "unbelieving" Thomas still had to be convinced personally (John 20:24-29).

Within earliest Gentile Christianity, the denial of the
resurrection even seems to have developed into a heresy
which found sufficient adherents so that Paul was forced
to devote a detailed chapter in 1 Corinthians (15) to its
refutation. Among other statements we read there,
"Now if Christ is preached as raised from the dead, how
can some of you say that there is no resurrection of the
dead?" (1 Cor. 15:12). If we add to all these disturbing
factors the statement that in the ancient world there
were not less than a round dozen of nature deities, heroes,
philosophers, and rulers who, all long before Jesus, suffered, died, and rose again on the third day, then the
skepticism of most non-Christians can easily be understood. For example, Joachim Jeremias reports on the
pagan resurrection "on the third day":

> Osiris dies on 17 Athys; the discovery and revivi-
> fication of his body follows in the night of the
> 19th; . . . The death of Attis is celebrated on 22
> March, his return to life probably on 25 March;
> . . . The day of the resurrection of Adonis is not

certain, but the third day is probable (op. cit., p. 304).

The Babylonian Tammuz, whose cult had spread to Jerusalem, the Syrian Adonis, the Phrygian Attis, the Egyptian Osiris, the Thracian Dionysos — to mention only the most important deities—all underwent suffering and martyrdom, some died on the cross. The death of some deities even had expiatory power. And in almost all cases their resurrection was connected with the hope for human immortality.

The imprisonment of the savior of the world, his interrogation, the condemnation, the scourging, the execution in the midst of criminals, the descent into hell —yes, even the heart blood of the dying gushing out of a spear wound, all these details were believed by millions of believers of the Bel-Marduk mystery religion whose central deity was called the savior sent by the Father, the one who raises the dead, the Lord and the Good Shepherd.

Herbert Braun, who points to the resurrection of Attis, Adonis, Isis and Osiris, Heracles, Pythagoras, Apollonius of Tyana, Alexander the Great, and Emperor Augustus, concludes that "the belief in the Resurrection is an early Christian form of expression, a form of expression conditioned by its environment, . . . which we shall not be able to regard as binding on us" (*Jesus of Nazareth, the Man and His Time*, tr. E. R. Kalin, Philadelphia: Fortress, 1979, p. 122f.).

Be that as it may, it had to appear to many contemporaries of the early church that the story of Jesus is basically no more than another mythology of a father of gods who lets his son die and raises him back to life in order to save his believers. And since this avalanche of objections was by no means sufficient rationally to bury faith in the resurrection, an imposing cardinal argument still attempts to refute it, an argument which the orator Celsus has already formulated in the second century, as follows: "If Jesus actually possessed divine miraculous power, why did he not appear also to outsiders and opponents and especially the people as a whole?"

Hermann Samuel Reimarus, whose essay "The Goal of Jesus and His Disciples" was edited by Gotthold Ephraim Lessing in the year 1778, presents a long chain of "contradictions" which seek to unmask the Easter faith of the disciples as a cunning fraud. There we read among others,

> Even if we had no other scruples concerning the resurrection of Jesus, the one that he did not appear publicly would be sufficient in itself to overthrow any plausibility; for it can never be reconciled with the purpose for which Jesus is supposed to have come into the world.

There never has been a lack of plausible historical objections which seek to deny any reality of that resurrection. But that which impairs these purely "logical" counter-arguments is the circumstance that they attempt to understand "reality" in a restricted way, exclusively as a physically comprehensible or rationally understandable facticity—a standard which is hostile to all human faith. It is a lack of empathy with the Jewish locus of that original Easter faith whose eyewitnesses and first testifiers were without exception sons and daughters of Israel.

Resurrection in Judaism

"Is Christ divided?" This provocative question of Paul to the Corinthians (1 Cor. 1:13) seems to be affirmed by many theologians nowadays. For they practice a clear division of the Nazarene into two — an earthly Jesus who is of no significance in regard to the history of salvation and a post-Easter Christ who is considered as the exclusive center of all doctrines of salvation.

The historical Jesus, so one says, was indeed born as a Jew, was circumcised, educated, and lived his whole earthly life among Jews, his ministry, preaching and teaching being limited to the physical nation of Israel. It is completely different with the post-Easter Christ who, as a heavenly figure of light or as a "Masked God," as Eduard Schillebeeckx ironically calls this construction, has nothing at all to do with his birth in Judaism or with our earth. In the words of Willi Marxsen:

> They say that the important matter is not the cause of Jesus but the exalted Christ . . . Jesus of Nazareth and the Christ must in no way be compared. But if the concern is decisively with Christ, then Jesus stands under a minus sign as does his own cause, the things he cared about, the things that were important to him (*Die Sache Jesu geht weiter*, Gütersloh 1976, p. 14).

The oldest reports in the New Testament about the resurrection of the Nazarene give the lie to this widespread opinion. Repeatedly they emphasize not only the bodiliness of the Risen One, but also his unbroken identity with the same Jesus of Nazareth whose life and strife was devoted to his people Israel. And finally, after his death on the cross, he appeared exclusively to Jews, for there are no Gentiles among the numerous witnesses of the Risen One. This applies to the three Marys and the group of apostles as well as to the disciples of Emmaus and "the more than five hundred brethren" of whom Paul speaks later on. Peter says to his fellow Jews in the portico of the temple in Jerusalem, "God, having raised up his servant, sent him *to you* first, to *bless* you" (Acts 3:26). This means that the Risen One came in order to bless Israel. The unavoidable conclusion that forces itself on us from these facts is that the Easter event, in whatever way one wants to understand it, was primarily and chiefly a Jewish faith experience. Easter faith came into existence—just as Jesus himself—in the midst of the people of Israel and spread from there over the whole world. In order to do justice to this Easter faith and to discuss its historical origin properly, it is therefore necessary to go back mentally into the time and environment of the Nazarene. Only a re-presentation of its Jewish setting can bring that resurrection in Jerusalem, which has become the birth certificate of the church, close to us.

The resurrection of Jesus can be proved—or refuted—only from Jewish sources since the Nazarene, both in his lifetime and after Good Friday, has ministered only within his homeland and his people Israel.

In order to do justice to that apostolic basic faith which has for more than one and a half millennia put its stamp on the history of the world, two preliminary questions must be clarified: (1) Was Judaism already before the time of Jesus acquainted with individual resurrections? (2) Was the hope of the resurrection from the dead already part of the Jewish faith in the time of Jesus?

The Hebrew Bible knows of the translation of Enoch (Gen. 5:24), a transfiguration (Saul: 1 Sam. 10:6) and an ascension (Elijah: 2 Kings 2:11) and of three resurrections or resuscitations which God had carried out through the hands of his prophets.

The first case concerns a devout widow at Zarephath whom God had commanded, at the time of a famine, to feed the prophet Elijah, which she was willing to do despite her great poverty. When she divided her last supplies with the prophet, God multiplied her meal and oil so that she, her son, and Elijah always had sufficient food during the famine. Then the Bible continues:

> After this the son of the woman, the mistress of the house, became ill; and his illness was so severe that there was no breath left in him. And she said to Elijah, "What have you against me, O man of God? You have come to me to bring my sin to remembrance, and to cause the death of my son!" And he said to her, "Give me your son." And he took him from her bosom, and carried him up into the upper chamber, where he lodged, and laid him upon his own bed. And he cried to the Lord, "O Lord my God, hast thou brought calamity even upon the widow with whom I sojourn, by slaying her son?" Then he stretched himself upon the child three times, and cried to the Lord, "O Lord my God, let this child's soul come into him again." And the Lord hearkened to the voice of Elijah; and the soul of the child came into him again, and he revived. And Elijah took the child, and brought him down from the upper chamber into the house, and delivered him to his mother; and Elijah said, "See, your son lives." And the woman said to Elijah, "Now I know that you are a man of God, and that the word of the Lord in your mouth is truth" (1 Kings 17:17-24).

The second case concerns a wealthy woman in the town of Shunem near Megiddo who received the prophet Elisha, the successor of Elijah, in her house and offered him a small roof chamber in her house, the "chamber of a prophet." In gratitude for her hospitality, Elisha predicted that this childless woman would bear a son who was born "about that time the following spring." After this incident we read,

> When the child had grown, he went out one day to his father among the reapers. And he said to his father, "Oh, my head, my head!" The father said to his servant, "Carry him to his mother." And when he had lifted him, and brought him to his mother, the child sat on her lap till noon, and then he died. And she went up and laid him on the bed of the man of God, and shut the door upon him, and went out. . . .
> When Elisha came into the house, he saw the child lying dead on his bed. So he went in and shut the door upon the two of them, and prayed to the Lord. Then he went up and lay upon the child, putting his mouth upon his mouth, his eyes upon his eyes, and his hands upon his hands; and as he stretched himself upon him, the flesh of the child became warm . . . the child sneezed seven times, and the child opened his eyes. Then he summoned Gehazi and said, "Call this Shunammite." And when she came to him, he said, "Take up your son." She came and fell at his feet, bowing to the

ground; then she took up her son and went out (2 Kings 4:18-21, 32-37).

The third resuscitation happened to an unknown man whose corpse came into contact with the bones of Elisha in the tomb so that the prophet, even after his death, was able to resuscitate a dead person to life.

So Elisha died, and they buried him. Now bands of Moabites used to invade the land in the spring of the year. And as a man was being buried, lo, a marauding band was seen and the man was cast into the grave of Elisha; and as soon as the man touched the bones of Elisha, he revived and stood on his feet (2 Kings 13:20-21).

All three resuscitations describe physical resurrections which are reported with significant sobriety. Not a single case seems to have met with unbelief in Israel or have led to any sort of supernatural consequences in the further life of the resuscitated persons.

Similar phenomena apply to the postbiblical rabbinical literature where we find reports about several miraculous healings (Hanina, Dossa's son; Eleazar; Rabbi; etc.); the division of the floods of a river (Rabbi; Pinhas, Jair's son); the victory of a just person over demons (Hanina, Dossa's son); a miraculous multiplication of bread (the wife of Hanina); a rainfall after prayer (Honi, the drawer of circles); two stillings of the stormy sea (Rabban Gamaliel and Rabbi Tanhuma); and a

number of resuscitations whose significance or meaning
for salvation, however, is limited intentionally, as it
seems. E.g., a midrash of Leviticus says,

> Antoninus the emperor . . . came to Rabbi; he
> met him as he was sitting with his disciples in
> front of him. Antoninus said to him; "Are those
> the ones of whom you speak so commendably?"
> He answered, "Yes . . . the smallest among them
> is able to resurrect the dead." After a few days
> a servant of Antoninus became sick unto death.
> He sent to Rabbi, "Send me one of your disciples
> that he will make this dead man live again." He
> sent him one of his disciples . . . this one went and
> found the servant prostrate. He said to him;
> "What are you lying there prostrate while your
> master stands on his feet?" Right away he moved
> and rose (Leviticus Rabbah 10[111d]).

The Talmud reports (Meg 7b) that two rabbis, Rabba
and Rabbi Sera, at one time got so drunk in honor of the
Purim festival of joy that Rabba unintentionally killed
his teaching colleague. As soon as he became sober the
next morning, he asked devoutly for God's forgiveness,
and then Rabbi Sera awoke to life again. When a year
later he invited Rabbi Sera again to celebrate Purim, the
latter declined with the words "a miracle doesn't happen
every time."

Among the miracle workers of the rabbinic tradition
to whom resuscitations of dead persons are ascribed are,

among others: Rabbi Shimon bar Yohai, Rabbi Hanina bar Hama, Rabbi Israel Baal Shem Tov, and Rabbi Schmelke of Nikolsburg who is supposed to have revived a woman who had died in childbirth.

Concerning the general resurrection of the dead, we find some allusions and hints in the Hebrew Bible, as for instance in the book of Job, where that hero of faith calls to his false friends, "For I know that my Redeemer lives, and at last he will stand upon the earth; and after my skin has been thus destroyed, then without my flesh I shall see God, whom I shall see on my side, and my eyes shall behold, and not another" (Job 19:25-27).

In a similar way the prophet Hosea appeals to his people in an allusion which is in even clearer language, "Come, let us return to the Lord; for he has torn, that he may heal us; . . . after two days he will revive us; on the third he will raise us up, that we may live before him" (Hos. 6:1-2).

Ezekiel was permitted to see in a unique vision the national, spiritual, and physical resurrection of all of Israel,

> Then he said to me, "Son of man, these bones are the whole house of Israel . . . thus says the Lord God: Behold, I will open your graves, and raise you from your graves, O my people; and I will bring you home into the land of Israel. And you shall know that I am the Lord, when I open your graves, and raise you from your graves, O my

people. And I will put my Spirit within you, and you shall live" (Ezek. 37:11-14).

Daniel received the promise of his own resurrection, "But go your way till the end; and you shall rest, and shall stand in your allotted place at the end of the days" (Dan. 12:13) and proclaims to us also the eschatological coming of the last judgment in which the just will rise to eternal life, but the unjust to condemnation, "And many of those who sleep in the dust of the earth shall awake, some to everlasting life, and some to shame and everlasting contempt" (Dan. 12:2).

The question of what remains of a human being after death is a riddle which has occupied Jews for millennia. The hope beyond death appears in its rudiments already in the Babylonian exile but does not gain ground until the times of the Maccabees. That was a period of unprecedented persecutions and religious as well as national oppression by the Syrian-Greek world of paganism which had begun a general attack against Judaism— and an unprecedented haven of refuge was sorely needed which only faith was able to provide.

While in earlier times patriots, priests, and prophets were in a position to declare any misfortune as a punishment from God for the evil deeds of Israel, now it was primarily a suffering of the devout, of those who held God and his law in high honors, while those that assimilated themselves—the Hellenists and the apostates who succumbed to the pagan cults—flourished.

"Why does the way of the wicked prosper? Why do all who are treacherous thrive?" This searching question of Jeremiah (12:1) was on the lips of all people in 168 B.C.E. when Emperor Antiochus had a pig sacrificed in the holy of holies and an altar to Zeus erected in the temple. This question also appeared in the thoughts of the psalmist who went even further:

> For I was envious of the arrogant, when I saw the prosperity of the wicked. For they have no pangs; their bodies are sound and sleek . . . therefore pride is their necklace; violence covers them as a garment. . . . Behold, these are the wicked; always at ease, they increase in riches. All in vain have I kept my heart clean and washed my hands in innocence. For all the day long I have been stricken, and chastened every morning" (Ps. 73:3-14).

This time it was not a general chastisement of the people which was considered in earlier periods by the devout as "purification." The pagan rulers also could not be considered as tools of the wrath of God, as in the times of Cyrus, because their selective persecution befell mainly those in Israel who were righteous and observed the Torah. Therefore, it became the solid faith of this tortured generation that the salvation and well-being of the righteous and the condemnation of the wicked would restore justice on earth as soon as the kingdom of God would come. The apocalyptic literature of those painful years is almost exclusively devoted to the manner and the time in which this longed-for fulfillment could be expected. But since the righteousness of God necessarily demanded that this justification should affect especially those righteous people who had sacrificed their life for the faith, all those "who sleep in the dust of the earth" must appear before the future judgment which would decide their fate forever, according to the earthly deeds of each person.

Basic biblical thoughts are essential for this theological development, such as the omnipotence of God over life and death, the confidence of God's righteousness which— even if hidden and humanly incomprehensible—should become apparent sooner or later for all people, and the hope for the end time in which the kingdom of God would lead all prophetic promises to fulfillment. It was obvious for believing Jews throughout the ages that such a crowning realization must include the return of all martyrs and the restoration of the total covenant people.

The historical fact that the resurrection of the dead was solidified into a doctrine of Judaism not until a relatively late time explains also its rationality. Unlike the mystery cults of Egypt, Greece, and Asia Minor which also believed in the resurrection, it is free from magic, mysticism, miraculousness, and lengthy burial rites, which often degenerated into worship of the dead.

If God is all-just and all-merciful, then death in this world cannot be the final end. This conclusion became the simple, irrefutable theo-logic for most people in Israel. Of more than historical significance is the fact that the small band of the Maccabees, for the first time in the history of biblical faith, believed solidly and imperturbably in the resurrection of the dead and thus were able to overcome the overwhelming power of enemies and to establish again an independent Israel after a subjection of more than four hundred years. Thus, the power of faith in a beyond proved itself an insuperable impetus for improving this world in faithfulness to the Bible.

All this happened in a clear refutation of the atheists and Marxists who designate all religion simply as "opium for the people" by which the believers are to be comforted with a beyond in order to accept, without change, the misery of this world. But it also may be the case, as most rabbis claim, that the faith in the resurrection of the dead is much earlier than the Maccabees, that it is as old as Judaism itself. In this respect, one midrash asserts that Abraham, when he was about to sacrifice his son Isaac at the command of God, did it because "He considered that God was able to raise men even from the dead" (Heb. 11:19).

"All of Israel shares in the future world" (Sanhedrin XI, 1 and Aboth I, 1) is one of the first obligatory statements of early rabbinic Mishnah, and since the Greek separation of body and soul was far from Jewish thought and the resurrection by God was usually considered as a return to the earth, purified from sin and evil, a bodily resurrection, even in regard to eternal life, was not an insoluble problem for most rabbis, even pre-Christian Judaism.

Resurrection also did not become such a problem when several Jewish circles inclined to consider the world as incurably evil and when, therefore, hopes for a new heaven and new earth were transferred to the resurrection life in paradise or in heaven. Any life in general was conceived of as bodily and spatial.

Another trajectory, influenced more by the thought of divine retribution, led to the conception of a general resurrection.

"The righteous of all nations of the earth share in the future world" (Sanhedrin X, 2). In the high Middle Ages, this was explicitly applied to all believing Christians and Moslems. A combination of both conceptions appeared in the doctrine of the two resurrections—one of all Israelites for the messianic kingdom, and, when this is accomplished, the resurrection of all people for judgment.

Thus Rabbi Joseph Javitz, a victim of the expulsion of the Jews from Spain, was able to write around 1495 C.E., "The Christians believe, like we do, in the creation of the world, in the patriarchs, in revelation, in retribution, and in the resurrection of the dead. Blessed be the Lord, the God of Israel, that he has left us this remnant . . . if there were not these Christian nations, our faith might have—God forbid—wavered."

The various conceptions of the resurrection in those

times—all people or only the righteous; on earth or in heaven; pre-messianically or eschatologically; etc.—resist any kind of systematizing. All schools have in common the belief that resurrection is a resuscitation of the dead, effected by God, without definitely answering the question of when, who, and where. Within the pluralism of Jewish faith, the spectrum of various expectations of the Messiah was—and is—just as broad as the scale of the hoped-for resurrection.

Similar statements apply to the exegetical democracy of the rabbis whose axiomatic principle was that inherent "in each Bible word, there are seventy different possibilities of interpretation." Already at the beginning of the first century, the two chief Pharisaic schools of Hillel and Shammai believed in the bodily resurrection (Genesis Rabbah XIV and Leviticus Rabbah XIV) and interpreted the most diverse scripture references in this sense. Just to give three examples:

> Our masters taught, "I kill and I make alive" (Deut. 32:39). One might think that one person would experience the killing and the other the making alive as it is customary in the world; but the text says "I wound and I heal" (Deut. 32:39). As wounding and healing applied to one and the same person, so also killing and making alive applied to one and the same person. This provides an answer for those who say that the resurrection of the dead cannot be proved from Torah (Sanhedrin 91b).

A few lines further down we hear of another example:
Rabbi Jehoshua, the son of Levi, said, How can the
resurrection of the dead be proved from Torah? Indeed
it says, "Blessed are those who dwell in thy house, they
will ever praise thee, Selah" (Ps. 84:4). It does not say:
They praised thee, but: They will praise thee. The revivi-
fication of the dead can thus be proved from the Torah
(Sanhedrin 91b).

The head of the school of the Pharisees adduced also a
proof from reason: "The emperor said to Rabban Gamaliel: You say that the departed will be revived. But
they turn to dust; and can dust be made alive? His
daughter said to him, let him be, I will reply to him:
There are two potters in our city. One makes pots from
water, and one makes pots from clay. Which of them is
more praiseworthy? The emperor said to her, the one
who makes pots from water. She said to him: If he is
about to make pots from water, should he not be even
more able to make them from clay?" (If God can create
people out of the drop of semen which is similar to water,
how much more can he do it from the dust of the dead?)
(Sanhedrin 90b/91a).

Faith in the resurrection was treasured so highly that
its deniers were considered as without salvation: "And
these are they that have no share in the world to come:
he that says that no resurrection of the dead is taught in
the Law, and he that says that the Law is not from
Heaven, and he that is a despiser of religion" (Sanhedrin X, 1).

Although later writings contain different views about the trespasses which deprive people of the hope of life beyond, the only passage that has canonical status is this anonymous passage in the Mishnah. It alone has become the subject of legal discussion and has led to heresy trials, to banning, and to excommunication.

Among the three groups which are denied eternal blessedness, the last refers to atheists, the second to sectarians, and the first—and most important—mainly to the Sadducees. This conservative elite group of priests, whose influence was restricted almost completely to Jerusalem, was theocentric in its doctrine, aristocratic in its world view, and pedantically literalistic in its understanding of the Scriptures: Whatever went beyond the literal meaning of the Bible was for them against the Scripture. And since the resurrection of the dead is mentioned nowhere in the Hebrew Bible explicitly, it was rejected by the Sadducces.

We may learn what the predominant circles of the Pharisees thought about this question when the Sadducees asked in dispute to which husband a woman would belong in heaven who on earth was married to seven brothers in succession in a Levirate marriage. [Naturally the question is intended to make faith in the resurrection ridiculous and is typical of the mockery of the Sadducees as we know it also from similar anti-Pharisaic controversy dialogues in the Talmud. For instance in p Yevamot 4:6b, the case is described where allegedly one of thirteen brothers by way of the same kind of

Levirate marriage married the twelve widows of all his deceased brothers.] Jesus answered with emphatic harshness, "Is not this why you are wrong, that you know neither the scriptures nor the power of God? For when they rise from the dead, they neither marry nor are given in marriage, but are like angels in heaven" (Mark 12:24f.).

Following this statement, Jesus combines, according to the widespread practice of the Pharisees, two different scripture passages in order to draw from them the conclusion which is indeed faithful to the spirit though not to the letter of the Bible. "And as for the dead being raised, have you not read in the book of Moses, in the passage about the bush, how God said to him, 'I am the God of Abraham and the God of Isaac, and the God of Jacob'? He is not God of the dead, but of the living; you are quite wrong" (Mark 12:26f.).

This is a reference to the often-repeated passage in Exodus 3:6 which Jesus brings into connection with Jeremiah 10:10 where it says, "But the Lord is the true God; he is the living God and the everlasting King." The words "the living God" can also be interpreted as "the God of the living." This somewhat free interpretation supports also the ancient tradition according to which the patriarchs, in the words of Paul, "had never tasted death" but were transported by God from this life into eternal life.

In his refutation of the superliteral doctrine of the Sadducees, Rabban Gamaliel in 90 C.E. overtrumped the

Nazarene by being able to combine *three* "proofs from Scripture" for the resurrection:

> The Sadducees asked Rabbi Gamaliel, "How can it be proved that God will revive the dead again?" He answered: "From the Torah, from the prophets, and from the writings. From the Torah: God said to Moses, 'Behold, you are about to sleep with your fathers; then you will rise' (Deut. 31:16, according to the Pharisaic reading!). From the prophets: 'Thy dead shall live, thy bodies shall rise' (Isa. 26:19, according to the Pharisaic reading). From the writings: 'May your palate be like the best wine that goes down for my lover smoothly, and makes the lips of the sleepers—(or: deceased) murmur' " (Song of Solomon 7:9) (Sanhedrin 90b).

What is then the connection between the verified individual resurrections in the Bible and the hoped-for resurrection of all the dead? Frequently the rabbinical demonstration relies precisely on the former in order to prove the latter. God's loving grace which he manifested in individuals guarantees, so to speak, the general hope for an afterlife. For instance, it says in a midrash on Ecclesiastes 3:15:

> God says, "I have said that I will revive the dead in the future," and humans ask wonderingly: "Should he be able to revive them again?" God answers them (the Sadducees!), "What do you

marvel about my desire to revive the dead? Have I not long ago revived dead bodies in this world through Elijah and Elisha and Ezekiel? That which will be has been in this world for a long time."

This faith was so deeply rooted in Pharisaism that Paul, without difficulty, was able to play off the Pharisees against the Sadducees when he had to defend himself in Jerusalem before the Sanhedrin:

> But when Paul perceived that one part were Sadducees and the other Pharisees, he cried out in the council, "Brethren, I am a Pharisee, a son of Pharisees; with respect to the hope and the resurrection of the dead I am on trial." And when he had said this, a dissension arose between the Pharisees and the Sadducees; and the assembly was divided. For the Sadducees say that there is no resurrection, nor angel, nor spirit; but the Pharisees acknowledge them all (Acts 23:6-8).

One and the same faith in the resurrection fulfilled here two functions: It was the precondition for the Damascus experience of Paul—and it brought some of the Pharisees to a recognition of the fact that this vision of the apostle to the Gentiles was willed by God: "Some of the scribes of the Pharisees' party stood and contended, 'We find nothing wrong in this man. What if a spirit or an angel spoke to him?'" (Acts 23:9).

Be that as it may, Jesus (and his co-Pharisees) succeeded in "silencing the Sadducees" (Matt. 22:34), for the
expectation of the resurrection became a common conviction already two thousand years ago and matured
soon into the confidence of salvation of all faithful Jews.

Thus it says in the Thirteen Articles of Faith of
Maimonides which are part of the regular liturgy of the
synagogue: "I believe with full conviction that there will
be a resurrection of the dead at a time which will please
the creator."

Three times a day, every devout Jew prays in the
Eighteen Benedictions:

> Thou, O Lord, art mighty for ever, thou re-
> vivest the dead . . . and keepest thy faith to them
> that sleep in the dust. . . . who orderest death
> and restorest life, and causest salvation to spring
> forth. Yea, faithful art thou to revive the dead.
> Blessed are thou, O Lord, who revivest the dead.

In the morning prayer of the Sabbath it says:

> He arouseth the sleepers and awaketh the slum-
> berers; he maketh the dumb to speak, setteth free
> the prisoners, supporteth the falling. . . . To thee
> alone we give thanks.

In the daily table grace we ask God, "May the All-
merciful make us worthy of the days of the Messiah and
of the life of the world to come."

"The fear of death is the mother of theology," the

Greek philosophers asserted already two and a half millennia ago, and innumerable doubters have babbled it after them until today. The rabbis are of the opposite opinion. If we were to ask them for an aphorism which in laconic brevity would do justice to their world view, they perhaps would say: Not believing in death as the final conclusion of existence is the father of all life affirmation. How else could we explain that the Hassidim on the day of the death of their rabbi dance around his grave —out of joy that he "returned home"; or that the rabbinical expression for "he has died" does not speak of deceasing but says simply, "he has gone into his world," an expression in which the "world of truth" which is meant can be translated only inadequately by "beyond"?

Thus it also is not an accident that in the Jewish prayer for the deceased — the Kaddish of "sanctification" — which every son prays daily for eleven months after the death of his father or mother, not a word is spoken of death, dying, mourning, or decease, but quite to the contrary: of the kingdom of God, of the praise of the Father in heaven, of his creation, of hope for salvation, of peace of the endtime, and, last but not least, of eternal life.

This certainty of a future resurrection of all and of a possible earlier resurrection of some people especially graced by God was the precondition of the Easter faith of the disciples whose faith experience, just as that of their Master, was influenced widely by Pharisaism.

They prove this unanimously in the first four different answers they give to the question of Jesus, "Who do men say that the Son of man is?" They respond: John the Baptist, Elijah, Jeremiah, or one of the prophets. All four opinions, which probably at that time were widespread among the population of the country, influenced by the Pharisees, presuppose the resurrection of dead Jews (reincarnated in Jesus) as self-evident.

The same Pharisaic confidence may also be heard in the words of Martha who emphasizes to Jesus, "I know that he (Lazarus) will rise again in the resurrection at the last day" (John 11:24).

If the apostles had been Sadducees, then Good Friday would have meant for them the extinction of all hope and the final breakdown of the Jesus movement. To speculate even more boldly—if they had been Buddhist, they would have understood the resurrection as a punishment of God since their final salvation would have to be sought in the nonexistence of Nirvana. As Gnostics they would have saluted Good Friday as Jesus' deliverance from the burdensome body, the prison of his soul, and probably would have cursed the physically risen Jesus (1 Cor. 12:3). Only because they were Jews educated by Pharisees was their solid conviction of resurrection the first step to their later Easter faith. Only because they were Pharisaic Jews was the indispensable foundation of their common confidence that this earthly life, despite all tortures and disappointments, was not meant for meaninglessness and that their master even in death was not deserted by the God of Israel.

Passover–Sinai–Golgotha

What do we know of the earthly Jesus of Nazareth? The findings of scholarship can be summarized in a few lines. In the words of Fritz Leist:

> Between the years of 9 B.C.E. and 4 C.E., a son was born to a carpenter in Nazareth, who, already in his early years, attracted public attention in Galilee with his preaching of repentance and his message of salvation. Within a short time, he found disciples who followed him and a growing circle of adherents, many of whom hoped that he would be the Messiah for whom Israel longed.
>
> Around the year 29 or 30 he went from Galilee to Jerusalem where he was crucified as a political rebel by the Romans, probably with the aid of

leading Sadducees, who considered the radical-
ness of his message as dangerous.

Albert Schweitzer attempts to reconstruct a different
possible course of the historical drama of Jesus with his
consistent eschatology. The chief mileposts in the earthly
career of the Nazarene are, in the words of this histori-
ographer of the quest of the life of Jesus, the following:

> In regard to the mission of the Twelve . . . Jesus
> . . . tells them in plain words (Matt. 10:23) that
> He does not expect to see them back in the present
> age. The Parousia of the Son of Man, which is
> logically and temporally identical with the dawn
> of the Kingdom, will take place before they shall
> have completed a hasty journey through the cities
> of Israel to announce it. . . . It is equally clear, . . .
> that this prediction was not fulfilled. . . . It should
> be noted that the non-fulfillment of Matt. 10:23
> is the first postponement of the Parousia. . . .

Soon after, in connection with Jesus' prediction of his
sufferings, he says,

> There followed neither the sufferings nor the out-
> pouring of the Spirit, nor the Parousia of the Son
> of Man. . . . In leaving Galilee he abandoned the
> hope that the final tribulation would begin of
> itself. . . . The movement of repentance had not
> been sufficient. When . . . he hurled the fire-
> brand which should kindle the fiery trials of the
> Last Time, the flame went out. . . . He placed his

Parousia at the end of the pre-Messianic tribulations in which he was to have his part. The suffering, death, and resurrection of which the secret was revealed at Caesarea Philippi are not therefore in themselves new or surprising. Questionable is only how Jesus imagined the succession of dying, rising, and Parousia as Son of Man. In itself it would be possible that he imagined the three events as happening in one act, perhaps in such a way that in dying . . . the supernatural course of events would begin and he would be revealed in his glory as Son of Man. The cry of despair on the cross (Mark 15:34) argues for this theory. The divine intervention which the Lord expected for the moment of the greatest need failed to appear (*The Quest of the Historical Jesus*, New York: Macmillan, 1964, pp. 358-389).

This also would explain the panic-stricken horror of the disciples which both Mark and Matthew describe as a headlong flight; either their master's death on the cross or the fact that at Golgotha a change of Jesus into the messianic Son of man did not take place could have instilled this clear feeling of failure in them. Probably they had expected such an event to happen on the basis of the predictions of his suffering.

Thus it is possible that the reason for their flight was not the event of his death but rather that which did *not* happen after his death on Golgotha.

Be that as it may, in both cases it would be the story of a prophet whose predictions repeatedly were not fulfilled; a movement of repentance which did not achieve its goal; and a faith community whose founder had to die a tragic death—as it repeatedly happened in the history of Israel before Jesus and also after him.

But how can it be explained that, against all plausibility, his adherents did *not* finally scatter, were *not* forgotten, and that the cause of Jesus did *not* reach its infamous end on the cross?

How could a proclaimer of salvation, three times disappointed, three times disappointing, become the starting point of the greatest and most influential world religion?

How was it possible that his disciples, who by no means excelled in intelligence, eloquence, or strength of faith, were able to begin their victorious march of conversion only *after* the shattering fiasco on Golgotha—a march which put all their successes before Easter completely into the shadow?

In other words: How did it nevertheless come about that the adherents of Jesus were able to conquer this most horrible of all disappointments, that Jesus, despite everything, became the Savior of the church, although his predictions were not fulfilled and his longed-for parousia did not take place?

The answer of the apostles was brief and unambiguous: The resurrection of Jesus from the dead.

A short time after that Passover festival—in any case at Pentecost—Peter and his friends were "filled by the Holy Spirit," as it says in the Acts of the Apostles—which certainly means that they learned to understand the cause of Jesus in a new way and manner which they described unanimously with the word *resurrection*.

I can imagine from the Jewish way of life of those times why they chose exactly this expression to describe their experience of Easter. Naturally, I cannot claim true knowledge here, but surely it is an intuition resting on a certain familarity with the environment of Jesus. First of all it has to be emphasized that the general mood in all of Israel during the Passover festival is permeated by a thirst for, and an immediate expectation of, salvation.

What are the basic features of the Jewish Passover Festival? Its leading motif is the commemoration of the saving deed of God at the Exodus from slavery. This deed of salvation which represents the starting point for the experience of Sinai and the later conquest of Canaan is not only to be perpetuated in the memory of the people, but is to continue to live—in complete re-presentation—from generation to generation.

The most important Torah text concerning the Passover Festival belongs to the prescriptions for the three central pilgrimage festivals in Deuteronomy. It takes a clear position in favor of the historical interpretation of the festival and commands the double rite of Matzoth and the sacrifice of the lamb:

> Observe the month of Abib, and keep the Pass-
> over to the Lord your God; for in the month of
> Abib the Lord God brought you out of Egypt
> by night. And you shall offer the passover sacri-
> fice to the Lord your God . . . at the place which
> the Lord will choose. . . . You shall eat no leavened
> bread with it; seven days you shall eat it with
> unleavened bread, the bread of affliction—for
> you came out of the land of Egypt in hurried
> flight—that all the days of your life you may
> remember the day when you came out of the
> land of Egypt (Deut. 16:1-3).

The Matzoth—the bread of affliction but also of lib-
erty—is without taste and hard. It is supposed to be hard,
in contrast to the luxurious fleshpots of Egypt, for the
way into independence took Israel through 40 years of
wilderness, hunger, and struggle.

The sacrifice of the lamb, the central and evidently
oldest rite of the Passover Festival, no longer is in existence since the destruction of the second temple. At the
time of Jesus, lambs were slaughtered in the court of the
temple in order to be consumed by many thousands of
pilgrims in the evening in the family circle. But today
it is represented symbolically by a bone of lamb at the
seder table, since this sacrifice already in biblical times
was understood as a sign of the eternal covenant. The

Haggadah reminds us here both of the covenant of Abraham "between the pieces of sacrifice" (Gen. 15:10) and of the reconfirmed covenant with all three patriarchs: "God heard our lamentation (in Egypt)—and he remembered his covenant with Abraham, Isaac and Jacob."

And Rabbi Mattithiah ben Heresh comments on this: "The blood of the Passover and the blood of circumcision are both the blood of the covenant for whose sake the liberation from Egypt was granted." Here the close connection between blood toll and election is emphasized anew.

"*You* are among those who have escaped from Egypt." This sentence is the center and the soul of the whole Passover ceremony—and thirty centuries of Jewish history of suffering have driven home this profound truth to each generation with unmistakable clarity. In the Haggadah the ritual adds this admonition:

> He has liberated not only our ancestors but has liberated also *us,* at the same time with them: For there is not a single enemy, rising against us in order to destroy us, from whose hand the Holy One—Blessed be He—does not redeem us.

And still more clearly: "This happens for the sake of that which the Lord has done to *me* when I left Egypt" —words that made it possible for every Jew for millennia to sense the omnipresent, gracious love of God as a personal hope for well-being and salvation.

The Book of Numbers (9:11) adds to the double rite
of the lamb and the Matzoth, also the bitter herbs.
"These bitter herbs which we eat, why does it happen?"
Thus asks the Haggadah—and answers: "It points to the
fact that the Egyptians made the life of our fathers in
Egypt bitter. Scripture also says: They made life bitter
for them by hard labor in clay and bricks and in all kinds
of work in the fields." This is a statement which has
never lost its personal relevance both because of the
physical consumption of "bitterness" and because of the
Jewish experience of suffering. Furthermore, there is the
addition of the four cups of wine which were prescribed
already in the Mishnah—according to the book of Exodus (6:6-7):

> I am the Lord, and I will bring you out from
> under the burdens of the Egyptians, and I will
> deliver you from their bondage, and I will re-
> deem you with an outstretched arm and with
> great acts of judgment, and I will take you for
> my people, and I will be your God.

The four gifts of grace are: the bringing out, the deliverance, the redemption, and the acceptance or election
in honor of which the four cups of red wine are drunk.
Interesting is the custom of quoting the first part of the
Hallel—the Psalms of Praise, 113-118—before the second cup and their conclusion with the fourth cup. They
combine thanksgiving and hope for salvation melodi-
cally.

That this theme of divine deliverance is centrally em-
bedded in the Passover Festival is demonstrated by the
fact that in the course of history more and more analo-
gous acts of liberation were interpreted as Passover occurrences. Already in the eighth century B.C.E., Isaiah
evidently saw in the miraculous deliverance of Jerusalem out of the hands of Sennacherib a new Passover deliverance (Isa. 30:29; 31:5). Later times moved this
occurrence explicitly into the Passover night in appeal-
ing to the wording of the biblical narrative:

> As the destroyer entered Egypt long ago, so "in
> the same night" God's angel went out in order
> to liberate Jerusalem through his punishing judg-
> ment and to snatch it away from certain destruc-
> tion.

But also the deliverance of the three young men from
Nebuchadnezzar's fiery furnace (Daniel 3), the liberation of Daniel from the lions' den, the revocation of the
royal edict concerning the genocide of the Jews in the
times of Haman (Esther 4:16 and 5:1ff.), the deliverance
of the people Israel from the dangers of pagan Hellenism
by the unbelievable victory of the Maccabees—all these
events, together with other biblical salvation events, were
put, already in pre-Christian time, into the Passover
night.

"Pasach" has the original meaning in Hebrew of "passing over." At first it was to remind the people of the
protective *passing over* of the destroying angel past the

houses of the Hebrews in Egypt and of the crossing of the Red Sea. This *passing over,* however, was soon spiritualized and deepened into the basic Easter theme of the Exodus from oppression into freedom; from sadness into joy; from death to eternal life.

Jesus' intention to celebrate his last *seder* in Jerusalem is expressed in John (John 12:1) who emphasized that Jesus had already arrived six days before the festival in the capital. However, Mark and Luke also stress Jesus' careful preparation for the festival (Mark 14:12-16; Luke 22:8-14): "I have earnestly desired to eat this passover with you before I suffer," he says to his disciples on the day of preparation (Luke 22:15). Behind the evangelist's somewhat awkward Greek, excellent Hebrew can be retrieved.

The leading motif of the festival is the remembrance of God's deed of deliverance at the Exodus from Egypt. This chief thought sounds forth in the words of Jesus: "Do this in remembrance of me" (Luke 22:19). This was a reminder of the divine deliverance which was imminent or fervently expected—in consonance with an ancient Passover proverb: "In this night we were delivered; in this night we will be delivered" (Mekhilta to Exod. 12:42).

Jerome, 300 years later, confirms this in his commentary on Exodus: "It is the tradition of the Jews to expect the Messiah at midnight (of the Passover)—at the very time at which the first Passover was celebrated in Egypt." No wonder that the Romans significantly reinforced their occupation forces in Jerusalem on the day of preparation of each Passover Festival, since they were justifiably afraid of messianic unrest on the festival of the liberation of the Jewish people, as Flavius Josephus emphasizes.

Be that as it may, the Gospels confirm that Jesus as a Jew, faithful to the Scriptures, celebrated the seder in the Passover night in Jerusalem, spoke the prescribed blessing over the "bread of affliction," vicariously for all table companions, broke it, ate of it, and distributed the remainder unto his disciples who consumed it "inclined," as it is fitting for freed slaves.

In the same way they drank the third of the four cups —the kiddush cup (compare 1 Cor. 10:16)—over which Jesus as the house father spoke the wine blessing and from which he gave all apostles to drink, as is customary until today among Jews, in order to give them a share in the blessing. Certainly they also ate from the bitter herbs, as the Torah commands, which had to suggest to Jesus the thought of the "labor pains of the Messiah." From a comment of Hillel, whom some reputable scholars count among the teachers of the young Jesus, we learn that the basic structure of the present Passover liturgy, which is considered the first and perhaps also the oldest festival of the Jewish year, was already current in Jesus' times.

A passage in the seder text begins with the words "in remembrance of Hillel" which reminds us of Jesus' words, "do this in remembrance of me" (Luke 22:19).

In any case they spoke at the end of the Passover meal the "Song of Praise"—the second half of the Hallel (Mark 14:26), also according to ancient usage which is mentioned already in an early Mishnah (Pesahim X, 5-7).

The Passover Hallel which consists of Psalms 113-118 was sung already by Moses and the children of Israel at the Red Sea, according to a very old tradition, and was later ascribed to practically all Israelite heroes of faith as a thanksgiving song for miraculous deliverance from anguish and death. Thus Deborah and Barak, King Hezekiah, David, Hananiah, Mishael, Asariah, as well as Mordecai and Queen Esther, are supposed to have sung it, a report which underscores its central place in the festal liturgy of the synagogue, especially as a part of the Passover celebration.

This central ritual of Jewish faith says among other things, "the dead do not praise the Lord . . . but we will bless the Lord from this time forth and for evermore. Praise the Lord!" (Ps. 115:17f.). "The snares of death encompassed me; the pains of Sheol laid hold of me; . . . then I called on the name of the Lord: 'O Lord, I beseech thee, save my life!' . . . For thou hast delivered my soul from death, . . . I walk before the Lord in the land of the living" (116:3ff.). "Precious in the sight of the Lord is the death of his saints" (116:15). "I shall not die, but I shall live, and recount the deeds of the Lord. The Lord has chastened me sorely, but he has not given me over to death" (118:17-18).

And when the Passover Hallel says "this is the Lord's doing; it is marvelous in our eyes. This is the day which the Lord has made; let us rejoice and be glad in it" (118: 23f.), then these words must sound like an indication from heaven for those who, despite all hopelessness, do not want to give up hope for a saving deed of God. After all, it has happened so often in the annals of Jewish sufferings and afflictions.

One of the Aramaic folk songs that Jewish people still sing on the Passover evening is called *Had Gadya* (A Little Nannygoat). The leading motif of this song is the death of death, the conquest of all mortality by the intervention of God—and that in Aramaic doggerel which reaches back to biblical motifs:

One little nannygoat,
Playful and young,
Which my father bought
For the price of a song!
And along came a cat,
And ate up the goat . . .
And along came a dog,
and bit the cat, . . .
And along came a stick,
And whacked the dog,
Which had bitten the cat,
Which had eaten the goat . . .
And along came a fire,
And burned the stick,
Which had whacked the dog,

Which had bitten the cat,
Which had eaten the goat. . . .

Then the water extinguishes the fire; an ox drinks the water, the butcher slaughters the ox, and the angel of death takes away the butcher; then God who judges all creatures destroys even the angel of death—so that the final verse then can say: "He (God) gave death's wages to the angel of death, because he had strangled the butcher . . ." (or the Son of man as it says in an old translation). The kid or nannygoat stands for Israel, which though oppressed and persecuted time and again after its Exodus, will ultimately be redeemed by God in the messianic age.

Even if today's folk song comes from the Middle Ages, it is, nevertheless, characteristic of the mood of the Jewish Passover Festival of all times in which the past deliverance blends with the future redemption in an eternal today, in order to make present in this way the life-giving love of God as a timeless, eternal event of salvation.

Commenting on this Passover song which begins with the death of a kid (nannygoat) and ends with the immortality effected by God, Hugo Bergmann wrote on October 7, 1973, one day after the outbreak of the Yom Kippur War:

On the last page of our Passover Haggadah, there are the words, "and there comes the Holy One, blessed be He, and slaughters the angel of death." The story of the Haggadah which begins with the deliverance of our people from the servitude in

Egypt ends in the great redemption of human-
kind and of the world, in the death of death. . . .
We have to learn to take seriously the concept
and the doctrine of the salvation of the world;
and the salvation is first of all a salvation from
death. What does this mean? Isaiah gives the answer which cannot be misunderstood in Chapter
25, verses 7-8, "and he will destroy on this mountain the covering that is cast over all peoples, the
veil that is spread over all nations. He will swal-
low up death forever, and the Lord God will wipe
away tears from all faces." Thus death is a "covering," a veil or web which God will take away
from the people (*Freiburger Rundbrief* XXV,
1973, p. 2).

But now back to the Passover Festival of the Jewish
table fellowship in Jerusalem and its divine service.

For our understanding of Easter is based essentially on
the festival pericope for Passover week which, since time
immemorial, has been read in all synagogues at this "time
of our deliverance," as the Passover is called in the Bible.
From the 37th chapter of the Prophet Ezekiel:

The hand of the Lord was upon me, and he
brought me out by the Spirit of the Lord, and
set me down in the midst of the valley; it was
full of bones. And he led me round among them;
and behold, there were very many upon the
valley; and lo, they were very dry. And he said
to me, "Son of man, can these bones live?" And

I answered, "O Lord God, thou knowest." Again he said to me, "Prophesy to these bones, and say to them, O dry bones, hear the word of the Lord. Thus says the Lord God to these bones; "Behold, I will cause breath to enter you, and you shall live. And I will lay sinews upon you, and will cause flesh to come upon you, and cover you with skin and put breath in you, and you shall live; and you shall know that I am the Lord."

So I prophesied as I was commanded, and I prophesied, there was a noise, and behold, a rattling; and the bones came together, bone to its bone. And as I looked, there were sinews on them, and flesh had come upon them, and skin had covered them; but there was no breath in them. Then he said to me, "Prophesy to the breath, prophesy, son of man, and say to the breath, Thus says the Lord God: Come from the four winds, O breath, and breathe upon these slain, that they may live." So I prophesied as he commanded me, and the breath came into them, and they lived, and stood upon their feet, an exceedingly great host.

Then he said to me, "Son of man, these bones are the whole house of Israel. Behold, they say, 'Our bones are dried up, and our hope is lost; we are clean cut off.' Therefore prophesy, and say to them, Thus says the Lord God: Behold, I will open your graves, and raise you from your graves, O my people; and I will bring you home into

the land of Israel. And you shall know that I am
the Lord, when I open your graves, and raise you
from your graves, O my people. And I will put
my Spirit within you, and you shall live, and I
will place you in your own land; then you shall
know that I, the Lord, have spoken, and I have
done it, says the Lord."

Is it just coincidence that the leading motif of this
prophecy is the threefold opening of the graves and the
four times repeated resuscitation of the dead which is
addressed to the "son of man"? Is it just coincidence that
in this way the festal pericope of the Passover predicts
the resurrection of Israel in physical expressions as an
imminent saving deed of God? Three examples may show
hows Jews at all times have reacted to this vision.

The mountain fortress Masada in which more than
900 Jewish men, women, and children preferred suicide
to a capitulation before the Tenth Roman Legion has
become a symbol of the power of faith in all of Israel.
Yigael Yadin, who a few years ago was able to restore
the remains of this last flare-up of Jewish resistance at
the time of the second temple, reported that this heroic
voluntary death took place on the eve of the Passover
Festival in the year 73 and that the only well-preserved
fragment of Scripture discovered under the floor of the
destroyed house of prayer, carefully rolled up, was
Ezekiel's vision of the resurrection of the dead bones.

Almost 1900 years later, on the eve of the Hitler catastrophe, Joseph Carlebach, the chief rabbi of Altona,

preached at Passover time on the same immortal message
of Jewish confidence:

> Ezekiel's vision of the resurrection belongs to the
> most powerful and grandiose utterances ever pro-
> claimed by human tongue. From this vision which
> we read on the Sabbath of Passover in the syna-
> gogue went out the blessed word which still to-
> day makes unnumbered hearts throb in hope and
> confidence. The Prophet sees a valley full of
> dead bones. Can they revive, these dead bones?
> And as the word of God rushingly goes among
> them and the bones rise up and sinews grow over
> them and flesh comes upon them and skin is cov-
> ering them, and as the Spirit of God goes into
> these dead bodies reviving them and every last
> one of them becomes alive—that, says the proph-
> et, is a picture of the Jewish people, of these dead
> bones, a picture of the whole house of Israel. . . .

We only have to add that the most hopeless struggle of
despair in the history of Jewish resistance—the rebellion
in the ghetto of Warsaw—began in the late afternoon
of April 18, 1943, exactly at the beginning of the first
Passover evening.

Let us summarize:

The Passover hope of approaching redemption, the
dream of victory over death, the comforting Psalms of
the Hallel, and Ezekiel's vision of the resuscitation and

resurrection of the dead bones—these four basic elements characterized the mood of the Galilean group of disciples on that Good Friday which, without doubt, had to become the most difficult crisis of faith for the Jesus community.

The MUST of the Resurrection

References to the valley of despair are not missing in the Gospels.

Both the so-called betrayal and suicide of Judas as well as the naive description of the "denial" by Peter, the meaning of the words "you will all fall away" (Mark 14:27), the panic and flight of the disciples into their Galilean homeland, even the fact that the disciples had no knowledge of where Jesus was buried since at the time of the burial they were on a hasty flight home—all this proves unambiguously that on Good Friday everything —truly everything—came to a sad ending; at least so it seemed to most of his friends.

When Jesus suffered the cruel death of a rebel on a Roman cross, many of his adherents must have been afraid that they had fallen prey to one of the many

proclaimers of salvation or pseudo-prophets—a failure
which they strove to correct by an immediate flight.
Thus certainly on Good Friday and on the Sabbath following, a partial, if not widespread, defection must have
taken place. Perhaps most of his disciples were even ready
to bury the whole matter of Jesus together with their
dead master. It speaks undeniably for the faithfulness of
the early tradition that the disciples later on retained that
shameful memory of their little faith.

They had recognized in Jesus the man of God who
would bring the beginning of the fulfillment of all of
God's promises. Now the great dream had come to an
end. The death of Jesus was for them the end of a prom-
ising beginning—it was the ruin of the kingdom of
heaven. In permitting this, God had rendered his judgment on Israel, and thereby on the whole world—including the disciples themselves.

And thus Peter says in deepest resignation: "I'll go
fishing." And the others, a pitiful remainder of seven
men, all that had been left of the great Jesus movement,
of the mighty movement of hope, said dejectedly: "We'll
come along."

Often a messianic movement, a prophetic storm and
stress, a new movement of liberation, ended in this way
—all too often mingled with blood—among these incorrigible optimists to which God gave the name of Israel.
When Rabbi Akiba, one century after Golgotha, was
led to his execution, again by Roman legionnaires, because of the same messianic faith, his flesh was combed

with iron combs . . . but willingly he accepted the yoke of the kingdom of God and prayed—in the midst of the most cruel tortures—the "Shema Israel" . . . after which the Talmud continues:

> Then his disciples said to him: "Our teacher, do not continue (your prayer), let it be" . . . but he continued to pray and extended the final word (our God is) ONE so long until his soul expired with this word. Then the servant angels before God said: "Is that the Torah and is that its reward?" . . . a heavenly voice came: "Hail to you, Rabbi Akiba, for you are destined for the life of the future world" (Berakhoth 61b).

Akiba and Jesus—both lived in God's teachings for all of Israel, and their common effort was the salvation of their people. They died at the hand of Gentiles as heroes of the faith, with the name of God on their lips.

If Rabbi Akiba was promised eternal life, was Rabbi Yeshuah not just as worthy to attain to the future world? Their disciples saw in the death of both—as soon as new hope was able to overpower their depression—neither a defeat nor the end, but the crowning of an exemplary life—and the beginning of a new life which is exalted above any death.

The developing tradition perpetuated the memory of both Akiba and Jesus, picturing them as noble and close to God, insofar as Judaism and Christianity in their different conceptions were able to do.

In Isaiah we read: "When he makes himself an offering for sin, he shall see his offspring, he shall prolong his days" (Isa. 53:10)—prophetic words which in the interpretation of the early church have predicted for Jesus, as the suffering servant of the Lord, numerous followers and eternal life.

Only a believing Jew can have a presentiment of the depth of despair which this group of disciples of Jesus had to suffer on Good Friday, similar to that of Job.

Did the cause of Jesus really end in failure?

Did the cross definitively refute any hope for the kingdom of God?

That must not be the case! That dare not happen! Many a heart must have cried out like this. For here more was at stake than the death of a proclaimer of salvation whose radiant confidence had infected a group of believers. They were not just concerned about consolation or the end of their own distress, but about God himself and the meaning of their life.

If this righteous one, whose life and death were so exclusively and completely devoted to his confidence of salvation, had to fail so miserably, where was the justice of God? As faithful Jews they would rather live with tortured bodies, humiliated and persecuted by the Romans, than with an unjust God. "My God, My God, why hast *thou* forsaken me?" thus he cried in his agony. No reinterpretation or ignoring would help here.

Only a Jew was able to cry like that, one who felt utterly abandoned and disappointed to death. And thus

the resurrection of Jesus became for his disciples on that
day of ruin a theological imperative which was demanded by their never completely forgotten confidence in
God—just as Job had dared to demand an accounting
from his God even when it had to be extracted out of
the abyss of despair.

Jesus *must* rise in order that the God of Israel could
continue to live as their heavenly Father in their hearts;
in order that their lives would not become God-less and
without meaning.

This categorical *must* was not the illusory wishful
thinking of a deceptive flight from the world which
conjures up for itself a mirage, but it was based on the
Jewish insight that the God who is willing to love and
to suffer with human beings cannot be a cruel despotic
God like the idols of the Greeks and Romans. The Jewish God does not dwell high in the heavens in order to
impose his will imperially on his subjects, but is a loving
Father God who permits retort. He is ready to bargain
with Abraham for Sodom and Gomorrah, according to
the custom of traders; Jacob can win from him his blessing after a long struggle; he accepts three times contradiction by Moses; he is a God against whom Jeremiah is
permitted to rebel and who repents of having desired the
destruction of Nineveh so that he is willing to change his
decision—even when by this action he embarrasses his
prophet Jonah publicly. It was just as legitimate and
necesssary for Peter and his friends to dispute with him
as it was for the patriarch of Israel who dared to argue

against his creator, "Shall not the Judge of all the earth do right?" (Gen. 18:25) and who also found response for his protest in heaven.

The categorical *must* of the resurrection which can be considered a part of the saving plan of God, therefore, was applicable only and alone to the small group of disciples of Jesus whose life it was able to change so that they became the founders of the church.

It was the same *must* which inspired that unknown Jew who in the midst of the inferno of genocide was able to write on a wall in the besieged Warsaw ghetto:

> I believe, I believe, I believe
> with a perfect faith
> in the coming of the Messiah;
> in the coming of the Messiah I believe.
> And even though he tarry
> I nevertheless believe.
> Even though he tarry,
> Yet, I believe in him,
> I believe, I believe, I believe.

What can crucifixion, concentration camp, and the barbarity of war accomplish against such a certainty of God which can say with Job, "Even if he slay me, nevertheless, my hope is in *him*"? (Job 13:15 in the rabbinic reading).

A few hours later, before sunrise of the "third day" after Good Friday, that undefinable Easter experience took place which we cannot explain further, which as such is never described in the New Testament, but which has carried its effect into the whole world, phrased either as Jesus' "being raised" or "rising" from the dead.

It is not without consequence that the oldest layer of tradition in the New Testament designates this resurrection of the Nazarene explicitly as a deed of God as both Paul and Peter declare unanimously, "whom he (God) raised from the dead" (1 Thess. 1:10) and "but God raised him up" (Acts 2:24). Jewish Christianity was, in good Jewish fashion, convinced that its Messiah did *not* rise by his own power but was revived by the Lord of all life.

That all has happened "on the third day," although the interval between the crucifixion of Good Friday afternoon until the dawn of Easter Sunday was hardly longer than one and a half days, has also an evidently biblical-Jewish reason. Only in the context of the Hebrew Bible does this expression of the apostles, which certainly is not meant literally, have its underlying significance for the history of salvation:

- "On *the third day* Abraham lifted up his eyes . . ." (Gen. 22:4).
- "On the morning of *the third day* there were thunders and lightnings, and a thick cloud upon the mountain . . ." (Exod. 19:16). This introduces the appearance of God on Mount Sinai.
- "On *the third day* Joseph said to them, 'Do this and you will live' " (Gen. 42:18).

- "And Jonah was in the belly of the fish *three days*" (Jonah 1:17)—before he was saved.
- "On *the third day* Esther put on her royal robes" (Esther 5:1)—after which Israel was saved out of its bitter affliction.
- Hosea says it most clearly, "After two days he will revive us; on *the third day* he will raise us up" (Hos. 6:2). The rabbis comment on this in the Midrash Rabba: "The Holy One, Blessed be his name, never lets the just stay in affliction longer than three days."

"On the third day" has nothing to do with the date or with the counting of time but contains for ears which are educated biblically a clear reference to God's mercy and grace which is revealed after two days of affliction and death by way of redemption.

Thus, according to my opinion, the resurrection belongs to the category of the truly real and effective occurrences, for without a fact of history there is no act of true faith. A fact which indeed is withheld from objective science, photography, and a conceptual proof, but not from the believing scrutiny of history which more frequently leads to deeper insights.

In other words: Without the Sinai experience—no Judaism; without the Easter experience—no Christianity. Both were Jewish faith experiences whose radiating power, in a different way, was meant for the world of nations. For inscrutable reasons the resurrection faith of Golgotha was necessary in order to carry the message of Sinai into the world.

Both are true faith experiences which—just as the existence of God, courage, or love—escape demonstrable facticity in order to disclose themselves alone to faith. It cannot detract from the kernel of experienced truth that this fact of faith later on—in accordance with the spirit of that epoch—was surrounded by a dense wreath of legends, although doubters of all times say with Faust —or rather sigh—"I hear the message, but faith fails me." Faust has many companions of disbelief who can draw their religious ammunition easily from the New Testament.

Certainly the glad tidings are not without textual incongruencies—if one forgets that the truth of faith and the reality of knowledge operate on two different planes which can be harmonized only by genuine sensitivity. No wonder then that the evangelists' contradictory reports of the resurrection have not been able to convince the skeptics, that agnostics write off all narratives as fairy tales of the nursery, and that the purely historical result for sober scientists is extremely meager. However, legends *can* also be bearers of truths, which by no means deprive the kernel of the narrative of its historicity, as any scholar of religion will bear out.

Traces of a Jewish
Faith Experience

In the *Fragments on Revelation,* we read in Martin Buber:

> The actual event of revelation does not mean that a divine content pours itself into an empty human vessel . . . we know no other revelation than that of the encounter of the divine and the human in which the human participates factually. The divine is a fire which melts the human ore, but what results is not of the nature of fire. The fire itself is not tangible, but its traces can be recognized. God's word is so hidden and yet so effective in the human word, God's truth is revealed in the weak, often distorted, human statement.

Under all the multiple layers of narrative embellishments and the fiction of later generations, the Jewish New Testament scholar finds such traces of authentic Jewish experience.

(1) According to all four Gospels, women are the first ones to find the tomb of Jesus open and empty. In a purely fictional narrative one would have avoided making women the crown witnesses of the resurrection since they were considered in rabbinic Judaism as incapable of giving valid testimony (compare Luke 24:11).

The distrust toward women's statements in matters of faith goes back to the Hebrew Bible where it says in an old midrash on the Book of Judges (13:8ff.) concerning the promised birth of Samson:

> Manoah said to the angel, "Until now I have heard it from the women that I am to have a son . . . but one cannot rely on the words of women; but now the word may come from your mouth, I would like to hear it; because I do not trust her words; perhaps she has changed or omitted or added something" (Numbers Rabbah 10).

A similar story applies to the matriarch Sarah who simply denied her disbelief in the birth of a son which was promised to her: "But Sarah denied, saying, 'I did not laugh' " (Gen. 18:15). On the basis of this passage it has been taught that women are unable to give testimony before a court (Yalkut Shimoni I, 82). Since, however, in exceptional cases (Rosh Ha-Shanah 22a) a woman was permitted to give testimony before court that a man had died so that his widow was permitted to marry again, it had to strike the disciples as irony that here women wanted to testify to the opposite, namely, the resurrection of a dead person.

(2) In addition there is the fact that the women at the empty tomb were in the greatest excitement, "for trembling and astonishment had come upon them." They even fled at first from the tomb "and they said nothing to any one, for they were afraid" (Mark 16:8). That one of the witnesses was Mary Magdalene "from whom seven demons had gone out" (Luke 8:2)—which might at least point to hysteria—was likely to decrease the believability of her reports. Therefore, no further explanation is needed when we hear that the first report of the resurrection met with deaf ears even in the circle of the first disciples: "But these words seemed to them an idle tale, and they did not believe them" (Luke 24:11).

The circumstance that the same women wanted to anoint the dead Jesus shortly after his burial, as Jewish custom demanded, proves that basically none of the disciples nor the women themselves, who were certainly even more inclined to believe it, expected his resurrection. It increases the credibility of the basic Gospel statements that neither this fact which would put all pre-Easter predictions of suffering in question, nor the appearances of the angels to the women which precede all male testimonies to the resurrection, were treated with silence.

It also has to be emphasized that nowhere in the most ancient reports is it asserted that the statements of the women and the empty tomb had brought anyone to faith in the resurrection. Even more eloquent is the silence of the evangelists concerning the resuscitation of the dead Nazarene. According to all New Testament reports, no human eye saw the resurrection itself, no human being was present, and none of the disciples asserted to have apprehended, let alone understood, its manner and nature. How easy it would have been for them or their immediate successors to supplement this scandalous hole in the concatenation of events by fanciful embellishments! But precisely because none of the evangelists dared to "improve upon" or embellish this unseen resurrection, the total picture of the Gospels also gains in trustworthiness.

(3) Nowhere in the oldest testimonies is the resurrection described as an undeniable event which disclosed itself to all people. It became a reality originally only for those who had earlier been familiar with the living Jesus, who had learned from him unconditional believing—not for everybody, least of all for unconcerned outsiders.

The subjectivity of its reality clearly can be discerned when Paul (1 Cor. 15:3ff.) mentions with impressive reserve and restraint only that his informants had seen the risen Lord:

> For I delivered to you as of first importance what
> I also received, that Christ died for our sins
> in accordance with the scriptures, that he was

buried, that he was raised on the third day in
accordance with the scriptures, and that He appeared to Cephas, then to the twelve. . . .

Eight linguistic items speak in favor of the fact that
Paul in this oldest faith statement about the resurrection
does not pass on his own thoughts but indeed "delivers"
what he himself has "received" from the first witnesses.

1. Vocabulary, sentence structure, and diction
   are clearly un-Pauline.
2. The parallelism of the three individual statements is biblically formulated.
3. The threefold "and that" characterizes the
   Aramaic and Mishnaic Hebrew way of narra-
   tion.
4. The "divine passive" of "being raised" para-
   phrases God's action of salvation in order not
   to mention God, in accordance with the Jewish fear of the name.
5. The Aramaic form of the name "Cephas," not
   Simon, as Luke gives it in the parallel passage
   24:34, sounds more original.
6. The double reference "in accordance with the
   scriptures" supports twice in three lines both
   the death and the resurrection of Jesus—as it
   probably corresponds with the faithfulness of
   the early church to the Hebrew Bible.
7. "The twelve" as a closed group of the first
   witnesses includes also Judas—this both agrees
   with the consciousness of Jesus to be sent to

all of Israel and contradicts the supposed suicide of Judas (Matt. 27:5).

8. Finally, the statement, which in its basic features is repeated almost in all later reports of
the resurrection, narrates the course of *four*
events which were understood as salvation
bearing: He died for our sins . . . was buried
. . . was raised . . . and appeared. . . .

May this number of four events not correspond to the
four paschal gifts of God's grace: "leading away (from
Egypt) ; the deliverance; the redemption; and the acceptance as the people of the covenant"—as they find their
tangible symbolic expression in the *four* cups of red wine
which play such a central role in the last supper of
Jesus?!

Although a reconstruction of the original wording
is hardly possible, this unified piece of tradition which
soon was solidified into a formula of faith may be considered as a statement of eyewitnesses for whom the
experience of the resurrection became the turning point
of their lives.

Only in later "reports," which easily can be recognized as secondary embellishments, are they generalized
into a public event. Still later, as a polemic, spiteful reac-
tion against those who denied the Easter faith, they were
objectified into a historical event which supposedly does
not need any faith to be considered as true. The fact
that the ambiguity of the resurrection, which brought

only the disciples to Easter faith but strengthened others
in their disbelief, has been retained in the basic statements of the New Testament testifies to an honesty
which makes the exaggerated miraculism of the post-
canonical authors the more questionable.

Nowhere is the event designated as a "miracle," as an
event of salvation, or as a deed of God, a fact which tends
to support the plausibility of the report for the disinter-
ested reader. We do not read in the first testimonies of
an apocalyptic spectacle, exorbitant sensations, or of the
transforming impact of a cosmic event.

Instead of an exciting Easter jubilation we hear repeatedly of doubts, disbelief, hesitation, and such simple
things as the linen cloths and the napkins in the empty
tomb, of a race to the tomb which ends as "idling" and
such sober statements as for instance "then the disciples
went back to their homes" (John 20:10), or "Peter . . .
ran to the tomb; stooping and looking in, . . . he went
home" (Luke 24:12), and "they went out and fled from
the tomb; for trembling and astonishment had come
upon them" (Mark 16:8). It sounds almost as if any
jubilant outburst should be dampened, more covered
than uncovered, and as if the truth of the event needed
no emphasis.

The Jewish reader who is trying to grope between the
lines back to the kernel of the matter is involuntarily
reminded of the appearance which was granted to Elijah.
God was neither in the "great and strong wind" which
"rent the mountains, and broke in pieces the rocks," nor

in the "earthquake," nor in the "fire," but in the "still small voice, in the silence which was gliding away," as Buber translates—which Elijah recognized right away as the forerunner of the voice of God (1 Kings 19:11ff.). Only in the later legends is the taciturn experience of the original witnesses supplanted by inventive verbosity.

But the Jew is also acquainted with the believing embellishment of the later narratives whose epic breadth seems to grow with the distance from the event. One example of such embellishment are the targums. The targums are translations of the biblical text into the Aramaic popular language which were made before the time of Jesus. They embellished this translation by paraphrastic statements, enlargements, and explanations. Another example is the midrash—that "investigation of the Scriptures" which frequently takes the biblical text only as the starting point for a plethora of moral teachings, homilies, legends, and tales, in order to deepen the Holy Scriptures and "to bring heaven closer to the community."

Both targums and midrash employ artistic freedom as a method of teaching in order to make those distant faith experiences of the ancestors not only actual but present in a tangible way and to make it possible for the community to experience, at least partially, the enthusiasm and emotion of the biblical heroes by melodious sound, embellishment, puns, and rhetoric.

In addition there is this tautness of the Hebrew sentence structure where the tight form knows neither

decorative words nor extravagance, but limits its report
—the Bible is concerned about succinctly reporting
events of salvation—to a laconic brevity which often
presents a challenge to elaborate, think further, and spin
out. One also must not forget the fact that the holy text
—and this applies to both testaments—was primarily
an orally transmitted statement. And the experience of
God in speaking can only be revived in a spoken retelling.

Jewish tradition is so conscious of this original spokenness of the Word of God that Scripture—even after the
pen began to replace the sound—was audibly articu-
lated. "Reading" means in Hebrew primarily "proclaim-
ing." The essential reality of the Bible was revived anew
in proverb, saying, hymn of praise, and gospel, wherever
a mouth proclaimed it in full faith and believing ears
heard it. But spokenness for the Jewish piety of the disciples, prophets, apostles, and their successors means primarily a constant retelling, enhancing, and supplement-
ing one's own insight, explanations, and illuminations.
This emphasizes the vividness and life power of the text
in that it grows organically by being handed down, and
it gains in breadth and depth.

In the Jewish retelling of biblical stories, the word
becomes a deed and the deed becomes an event which is
relived by hearing, since word, deed, and event in Hebrew are expressed by one and the same term—*dabar*.
For the outsider these words which were written down
finally as a canonical text may look like a chimera, filled
with inconsistencies and contradictions, while the em-

phatic scientist of religion recognizes in it a woven texture of different faith reflections. Usually it turns out that historically questionable formulations become theologically understandable, and generous additions, after closer critical questioning, are based on the solid foundation of genuine faith experience.

Often does "a whole mountain of interpretations hang on a hair" (Hagigah 10a) of a brief scripture passage, as it is the case with the creation of Adam. The Book of Genesis devotes to it only a few brief sentences, but the midrash draws from it a plethora of instructive conclusions, only some of which can be quoted here:

> God created man not until the last day of creation. Why did He not create him on the first day?
>
> In order that later on no mouths can be found which spread the rumor that God did not create the world alone; that Adam had helped him.
>
> He also created him as the last in order that man not be arrogant. God said to him: "Do not forget that even the least living being, even the worm was created before you!"
>
> It would have been within God's potentiality to create more people at once. Why did he create Adam all by himself? If God had created more human beings at once, then the descendants of later generations would have boasted, "my father was nobler than yours."
>
> Therefore God created only one human being

in order that all descendants in the future should know that they have a common father, that they are all descendants from one father, and none of them belong to a higher or lower race.

God created all living beings through his word, but he created man with his own hands. For this purpose he took earth from the four corners of the world in order that man should feel at home everywhere.

And why did God create man in his image? In order that man should build further in the world and should do the work which God had begun before him.

Man was created as an individual in order that we learn that he who destroys a human being is as if he had destroyed the whole world—but whoever saves a human being is as if he had saved the whole world.

Adam was created as a single being in order to proclaim also God's greatness, for man imprints many coins with one form, and they all are alike, but the king of all kings, the holy one, praised be he, imprints each human being with a form of the first Adam, and, nevertheless, none is like the other.

Similar statements apply also to the *dust* from which man was made:

It says, "I will make your descendants as the dust of the earth" (Gen. 13:16). As the dust of the earth is from one end of the world to the other, so your children will be scattered from one end of the earth to the other.

As the dust of the earth is blessed only by water, so Israel will be blessed only by the merit of the Torah which is compared with the water. As the dust attacks the vessels but remains eternally, so also Israel. All nations of the world pass away, but Israel remains. As the dust is stepped on, so your children will be stepped on by the powerful; for its says: "you have made your back like the ground and like the street for them to pass over" (Isa. 51:23). But this is for your benefit, for they cleanse you from your sins, as it says "soften it with showers" (Ps. 65:10).

Known to all is the pensive narrative of Isaac's near sacrifice by his own father, Abraham, which has many meanings but to whose kernel the Bible devotes only four sentences.

When they came to the place of which God had told him, Abraham built an altar there, and laid the wood in order, and bound Isaac his son, and laid him on the altar, upon the wood. Then Abraham put forth his hand, and took the knife to slay his son. But the angel of the Lord called to him from heaven, and said, "Abraham, Abraham!" And he said, "Here am I." He said, "Do not lay your hand on the lad or do anything to him; for now I know that you fear God, seeing

you have not withheld your son, your only son,
from me." (Gen. 22:9-12).

This sparse description of the temptation of our father Abraham, his blind obedience, God's intervention
in the last possible moment, and the recognition of his
unquestioned power of faith—all this incited numerous
generations of Jewish interpreters of the Scriptures to a
never-ending, constantly new questioning of the text
since the greatness of soul of the two patriarchs and the
timeless significance of their willingness to sacrifice, constantly challenge them to get to the bedrock of meaning
inherent in the Holy Scriptures.

And so, in the course of time, an extensive treasury of
faith came into existence which built up the succinct
report of the Bible into a conglomeration of various faith
motifs. Only some fragments can be quoted here:

> Again the day had come on which the hosts of
> heaven gathered before God. Among them there
> was also Satan. God asked him: "When you visit-
> ed earth, did you see Abraham also? Did you
> notice how God-fearing he is?" Satan answered:
> "No wonder! He serves you only because you
> fulfill all his wishes. Just now you have given
> him a son in his old age. Just try to demand of
> him to offer this son to you as a burnt offering.
> You will see that he will refuse to obey your
> command."
> Then the word of God came to Abraham:

"Take your son and offer him to me as a burnt offering." Then Abraham said: "I have two sons and I don't know which of the two I am supposed to take." Then God said: "Take your son, your only one." Then Abraham: "Both Isaac and Ishmael are the only sons of their mothers. Sarah bore Isaac for me, and my maid Hagar bore Ishmael for me." God said: "Take your son, the only one whom you love." Then Abraham answered: "Both Isaac and Ishmael are dear to me in an equal way." Then God said: "Take your son, the only one whom you love—Isaac—and sacrifice him to me on the mountain which I shall show you."

When Abraham and Isaac were on the road, Satan made every effort to divert both of them from their undertaking. At first he changed into the form of an old man and said to Abraham: "I see that you are leading your son to sacrifice. Are you completely insane, did you become crazy? How can a father be so cruel?"

But Abraham recognized right away that this was Satan. He scolded him, shouted at him, and Satan disappeared.

Then Satan changed into the form of a beautiful young man and addressed Isaac: "Don't you know that this old dumb senile man who calls himself your father is leading you to slaughter? Why should you die in the bloom of your years? You still have the whole beautiful world before you. Flee from here!"

But Isaac replied: "God's command and my father's will are a guiding star for me."

When Abraham had arrived at the top of Mount Moriah in Jerusalem and wanted to sacrifice his son, Abraham stretched his hand and took the knife in order to slaughter his son. Isaac replied and said to his father: "My father, tie my hands securely so that I do not in the hour of my pain resist and disturb you, and your sacrifice might be found unsuitable."

The eyes of Abraham turned toward the eyes of Isaac, and the eyes of Isaac looked into the eyes of his father. In this hour the angels high in heaven came out and said to each other:

"Come, see, the only two righteous ones in the midst of the world. The one sacrifices and does not hesitate—and he who is being sacrificed willingly puts forth his neck."

This expansion of the original text is by no means the private endeavor of some gifted midrash scholar. Rather this text comes from the Jewish synagogue service as it was conducted also by the early congregation of Jesus. For when Aramaic had become the Jewish everyday language, already before the time of Jesus, no longer did all Jews understand the Hebrew mother tongue of the Bible. Therefore, the biblical text in the synagogue had to be translated into the popular language at which occasion the official interpreter attempted to make the text as lively as possible by letting the legendary treasure of the rabbinic midrashim flow into his interpretation.

The fact that neither heavenly voices nor miraculous deeds nor angels nor other celestial visions were missing did not detract from the believability of the expanded interpretation. On the contrary, the believing listeners were not as concerned about facticity as we are today and did not insist on historical precision as modern westerners do who are educated in a Greek fashion. So it assisted them to gain a better grasp of the "metaphysical" meaning of the narrative, for which all concrete points are merely means of grasping intuitively the saving truth behind the things.

Thus the original biblical text of Isaac's near sacrifice and the rabbinical expansion of the same event stand in a very similar relationship to each other as the oldest testimony of the resurrection of Jesus which in four short sentences (1 Cor. 15:3-7) wants to say the same as the fourth evangelist, two generations later, expressed in a midrash-like manner in two long chapters—namely: Here God has intervened, against all appearance and in spite of all unbelief, and revealed his power to save.

To blame the rabbis and evangelists for deception or to accuse them of lying would have been as foreign to the Jews and Jewish Christians of that time as an accusation of "embellishment" against Van Gogh or of the corruption of history against Shakespeare's *Macbeth* would be to us. The best proof for the solid faith in the resurrection is probably the realistic way in which the two oldest Gospels describe the painful death and Jesus' cry of despair on the cross: "And Jesus uttered a loud cry, and breathed his last" (Mark 15:37).

The Dominican Father Gonsalv Mainberger, in his Good Friday sermon "Did Jesus Die in Vain?" (preached in 1968 in the St. Jospeh Church at Lucerne) investigated carefully the question "For what purpose did Jesus die?" As a first possibility he examined and rejected the answer, "Jesus suffered and died in order to gain something." Then he continued: "There is a second answer, 'Jesus died in despair . . .' The despair is sounded in the last words of Jesus when he cried, 'My God, why hast thou forsaken me?' The despair also would be a possible end" (*Freiburger Rundbrief* 1967, p. 87).

In the words of Eduard Schweizer: "Without any euphemism Mark depicts the harshness of Jesus' death, recording only the single outcry 'My God, my God, why has thou forsaken me?' and stating that Jesus died 'with a loud cry'" (*Jesus,* p. 132). Joseph Klausner is of a similar opinion:

> The messiah crucified! the "Son of Man" hanged (and so become "a curse of God") by uncircumcised heathen and yet no help from on high! The great and gracious God, . . . his own heavenly Father came not to his help nor released him from his agony nor saved him by a miracle! . . . In his terrible anguish of heart he summoned up all his remaining strength and cried out, in his mothertongue, in the language of the book he loved

most: "My God, my God, why hast thou forsaken me?" Matthew and Mark preserve . . . the
very words. . . . It is, on the whole, unlikely that
the Church would have put such a verse in the
mouth of Jesus if he had not uttered it: The verse
is at variance with the Christian belief concerning Jesus and his sufferings (*Jesus of Nazareth*,
New York: Macmillan, 1953, p. 353f.).

It is difficult to refute the weight of this argumenta-
tion. For fundamentally, the whole New Testament is
nothing but a single grandiose effort to unriddle the
death of Jesus in the sense of faith. It never would have
been written if there were not the painful mystery of his
death. It speaks both in favor of the honesty and of the
strength of faith of the first Jewish transmitters that
this death, which seemed so senseless and in vain, could
be described originally with such simple and despairing
words. For only a sworn enemy of Jesus can describe the
end of his life in such a brutal, concrete way—or men
who are deeply convinced that this miserable dying of
the Nazarene neither was nor is the last word of God—
that his exit from this world became the entrance into
blessedness.

Erroneous Translations?

We also may assume that at least a part of the contradictions in the Gospel reports of the resurrection is based on errors in the translation of their Semitic original texts and models.

From numerous passages of the Greek New Testament, whose enigmatic character or implausibility can be alleviated, if not solved, by retranslation into Hebrew, we know that there must have been presynoptic reports about Jesus—written and oral—within the Jewish primitive church. The Greek evangelists were sufficiently familiar with neither the Semitic native tongues of Jesus (Hebrew and Aramaic) nor his Jewish environment. Two erroneous translations concerning the place and time of the resurrection appearances may support this supposition.

The location of the resurrection appearances was Galilee according to Mark and Matthew; Jerusalem according to Luke. Some scholars explain the Galilean appearance of Jesus from an old error of Mark which would have removed the fatal contradiction if other scholars had not spoken of a doubtless and even intentional error of Luke. Beyond that, neither Mark nor Matthew speaks of appearances in Jerusalem nor does Luke mention any in Galilee; and in the Acts of the Apostles, also ascribed to Luke, the Risen One charged the disciples explicitly "not to depart from Jerusalem, but to wait for the promise of the Father" (Acts 1:4). Luke thus is familiar only with appearances in and near Jerusalem; he does not know anything about appearances in Galilee.

This contradiction comes closer to a solution if we remember that "Galil" and the feminine form "Galilah" in Hebrew mean nothing but environs, region. Since Isaiah 9:1 which speaks of the "area of the Gentiles" *(Galil Hagoyim)*, one indeed is accustomed to designate the northern mountain province as "Galilee" which comes close to the Greek transcription of "Galilah." However, Ezekiel 47:8 knows a "Galilah Kadmonah" (eastern region), which corresponds to the area east of the temple place in or near Jerusalem.

It is highly probable that this designates the area of Bethany which was well familiar to the disciples as the city of Mary and her sister Martha (John 11:1), as a resting place after the celebrated entry into Jerusalem

(Mark 11:11), as the place of the resuscitation of Lazarus (John 11:43f.), and as the place of the anointing of
Jesus (Matt. 26:6-13 par.).

This "area of Jerusalem" *(Galilah Yerushalayim)* evidently confronted the later Greek-speaking evangelists
who were not familiar with the topographical designa-
tions of their Jewish sources with a riddle which Luke
attempted to solve by placing the appearances of the
Risen One in Jerusalem, Matthew and John, however,
in Galilee. This hypothesis gains in plausibility both by
the reference of Tertullian (second century in his *Apol-
ogeticum* to "Galilee, an area in Judea," and through
the common use of the word "Galil" in modern Israel
for the designation of any region.

This solution of a misunderstood "eastern region" near
Jerusalem would correspond well with the supposed
whereabouts of the disciples on Easter Sunday, as also
with the charge of Jesus to the apostles not to leave
Jerusalem before Pentecost. One might still add that
Jerusalem as the city of the last teaching of Jesus, his
crucifixion, and the expected parousia (Acts 1:11)
would also be the most plausible place of his resurrection
appearance.

Similar things may be said for the time of the resurrection. Matthew puts it at night, right after the end of
the Sabbath, but Mark and Luke in the early Easter Sunday morning. The obscure formulation of Matthew,
which is awkward in Greek (28:1) "now after the Sabbath, toward the dawn of the first day of the week (or:

of the Sabbath): or, according to the Elberfeld translation, "Late on the Sabbath in the dawn of the first day of the week . . ." seems to be based on an idiom current in Mishnah Hebrew: *Bemotzaei-Shabbat* or *le-ehad be-Shabbat* which means literally: "At the end of the Sabbath in the light toward the first day . . . ," but which, by means of a euphemism (light = night) intends to say nothing else but: "at the end of the Sabbath, in the night before Sunday." Basic is the fact that the Sabbath since Genesis 1:5 begins on Friday evening and ends on the next evening just as each new day lasts "from evening to evening" (Lev. 23:32). Unfamiliarity with this Hebraism seems to have led to contradictory statements of time in the Gospels.

The dejection of the disciples since Good Friday speaks in any case in favor of a visit to the tomb as early as possible, i.e., at the beginning of the night which coincides with the end of the Sabbath as is testified by the retranslation into Hebrew of the passage which is so obscure in Greek.

The Pedagogy of God

Two circumstances seem to confirm all disbelief: the nonpublic manner and the unoriginality of the resurrection.

Already in the second century, the rhetor Celsus posed the former as a basic question which must have confused many a new Christian of the early church: "If Jesus indeed had divine power to perform miracles, why did he then not also appear to outsiders and to opponents, and especially to the whole people?"

The nonpublic character of that resurrection caused doubts in the truth of Christianity which have not yet been silenced. Hermann Samuel Reimarus in his *Resurrection History* (published posthumously in 1778 by Gotthold Ephraim Lessing), writes:

> ... even if we had no other quandary at the resur-
> rection of Jesus, this one alone—that he did not
> let himself be seen publicly—would be sufficient
> to overthrow all believability; because this can
> never be combined with the purpose for which
> Jesus is supposed to have come into the world.

This objection, however, is not bothersome to any
scholar of religion.

The fact that this resurrection had only a few witnesses is no obstacle but rather a further proof of its
genuineness. That which the prophet Daniel reports concerning his revelation is basically valid for all prophets
of Israel, "And I, Daniel, alone saw the vision, for the
men who were with me did not see the vision" (Dan.
10:7). If we had been present on Easter Sunday in Jerusalem, we probably would not have fared better.

The Acts of the Apostles also testifies to the fact that
faith experiences have also been the special gift to clairaudient individuals or small groups. Acts emphasizes that
the risen Jesus did not appear to all inhabitants of Jerusalem and especially not to "all of Israel," but "to us
who were chosen by God as witnesses" (Acts 10:41).

If Jesus had appeared to all, or to many of his Jewish
contemporaries, in that feverish climate of expectation
of the imminent advent of the Messiah that permeated
all of Israel, then there would have been the possibility
that the Jesus movement and the church which followed
in its wake would have remained an intra-Jewish

institution—as indeed was the case in its initial years—without the message of the one God and his gracious love being carried into the world of the Gentiles.

But finally, it was faith alone that enabled people to experience what the apostles called the resurrection. And faith is not knowledge, but is a certainty which only true faith can grant. This is valid not only of Easter but of all foundational faith experiences in both Testaments.

If science and religion could be identified, where would the risk of faith remain? Faith is basically a "believing-in-spite-of"; it involves the courage to endure and conquer all doubts. By faith we entrust ourselves to the truth which is willing to forego all guarantees of tangibility. Neither the mystery of God nor of love, faith, and hope can be solved by equations—an impossibility that believing people affirm with their whole heart. For the desire to make faith secure is nothing but unbelief which is clinging to earthly materiality. The God in whom Jews and Christians believe can neither be couched in words nor defined by visible realities, for according to Karl Jaspers, "a proven God is no God," and this is true also of many of his deeds of salvation.

"I will not be inquired of by you" (Ezek. 20:3) applies both to the Lord of the universe, to his manner of revelation and his ways of salvation whose unsearchableness Isaiah, the psalmist, and Paul underscore explicitly. In the words of Eduard Schweizer, "Proof cannot be given of Jesus' resurrection. Here, too, very much as in the crucifixion of Jesus, God exposes himself to scepticism, doubt, and disbelief, renouncing anything that would compel men to believe" (*Jesus*, p. 49).

True faith experience has never been a mass phenomenon but the special gift of a few, of the clairaudient, of the metaphysically gifted, and of the sensitive. None of the great religions of our earth started as a mass movement. It was always unique individuals, a handful of seers, as the Hebrew Bible calls them, who saw what was hidden behind the mere facts, who had eyes not only for the crude, tangible events, but were able to comprehend events in order to disclose their meaning for a believing interpretation.

Why did God choose Moses, a person who was not eloquent and even stammered, to liberate Israel from the hand of the Pharaohs? This was the question of the rabbi of Mohilev—which he answered himself as follows: "The Eternal One has chosen intentionally a stutterer to proclaim his message in order that everybody may see that that which Moses had to tell did not come from his own eloquence but is God's own word." Abel, Noah, Isaac, Jacob, and Joseph, to name just a few, proved that God loves the weaker ones and that he puts the key to his miracles frequently into the hands of the humble and little ones—perhaps as an admonition that promise and fulfillment happen "not by might, nor by power, but by my Spirit, says the Lord of hosts" (Zech. 4:6).

Thus the Eternal One appeared only to Abraham; Jacob is alone when he struggles with the angel of the

Lord, nobody but Moses sees the burning bush, and
Elijah—in complete loneliness—hears the voice of God
neither in "a great and strong wind which rent the
mountains . . . nor in any earthquake . . . nor in the
fire . . . but in a still small voice" (1 Kings 19:11ff.).
In the same way all resurrections and resuscitations of
which the Bible and the rabbinical literature speak
happen only in the presence of individuals or a few
people who are personally concerned.

Thus the small number of the witnesses of the resurrection of Jesus is not an obstacle to the Easter faith
but, on the contrary, it speaks for the authenticity of
that salvation experience in Jerusalem almost two millennia ago.

Those that are pragmatic historians may say, well
that's good, but how is it with the resurrections of
Osiris, Attis, Adonis, and Isis, which are much older
than the church and were able to inspire millions of
Gentiles centuries before Jesus?

Indeed a weighty objection!

If resurrection is not an "invention" of the Bible
religions, but, as already indicated, an essential com-
ponent of most mystery cults and nature religions, is it
then not possible that the reports of the resurrection
of Jesus are just imitations of similar heathen myths?
Is this "unoriginality" of the Easter event not a telling
proof against its authenticity?

The Jew finds an answer of faith to this objection in
Maimonides (1135-1204), that greatest religious philo-

sopher of Judaism, who has had a lasting effect not only on his coreligionists, but also on Christian scholasticism and especially on Thomas Aquinas, through his master-piece *Guide of the Perplexed*. As the title of the book indicates, it is his concern to assist the doubters and undecided people in the attempt to reconcile faith and knowledge, religion and philosophy on a biblical basis. In the third part, which is concerned with the animal sacrifices in the preexilic temple, we read:

> If you contemplate the works of God . . . the planful process becomes obvious to you . . . the gradation in the various movements. . . . It is im-possible to go immediately from one extreme into the opposite. . . . Therefore the human being, ac-cording to nature, cannot give up what he or she was used to do. . . . God sent our teacher Moses in order to make Israel through the knowledge of God into a kingdom of priests and a holy people. . . . At that time the general worship of God con-sisted in . . . sacrificing certain kinds of animals, in prostrating oneself before images, and in offer-ing incense to them. . . . Therefore God's wisdom did not command us to relinquish all these kinds of worship, for because of the human nature which is always inclined to this which is custom-ary, it would have been something which nobody would have wanted to accept. . . . And therefore God permitted these kinds of worship to continue . . . and transferred them to his name. . . . This

wise institution (of temple, altar, and priests) succeeded in eliminating idolatry . . . and establishing the teaching of the Oneness of God in our faith without repelling or deterring the souls by this. . . . And what would have hindered God to command us what he wanted at first? . . . Listen to my answer: something similar occurs already in the holy scriptures: "God did not lead them by way of the land of the Philistines . . . God led the people round by the way of the wilderness toward the Red Sea" (Exod. 13:17f.) . . .

And thus, as God, out of regard for their fear of something which they according to their nature could not endure, made them deviate from the right way which had originally been intended in order to achieve his *first* purpose in a *different* way, so he commanded sacrifices in order to achieve his *first* purpose, namely, the knowledge of God and the omission of idolatry, with regard to the fact that their soul did not have the ability to accept this immediately. . . . Just so it is not in the nature of human beings to give up the numerous kinds of worship of gods all at once. . . .

In view of this "pedagogy of God," would it not be possible that the Lord of the universe used the myth of the resurrection (which was well known to all pagans) in order "to eliminate idolatory in the pagan world" through the true resurrection of a just person and to carry "the knowledge of God" to the four corners of the earth by means of the Easter faith?

The "Lesser of Two Evils"

The resurrection of Jesus on that Easter Sunday and his appearances in the following days were purely Jewish faith experiences. Not one Gentile saw him after Good Friday. Everything that the Gentile church heard about the resurrection came only from Jewish sources because he appeared after Easter Sunday as the Risen One exclusively to Jews. Based on this historical fact, scientific analysis suggests three possibilities:

(1) The resurrection was a historical event that took place in the framework of this world and in the time of the first century in Jerusalem. That would be the first possibility. It has to be decided whether such an event, after such a long time and after the accretion of many layers of legends, is at all recognizable—or whether it remains covered up to the point of irretrievability.

123

(2) The second possibility is that the resurrection is a religious myth—as in all the mystery cults of the ancient Orient; a mythically colored legend, lacking any reality. In the half-mocking words of Friedrich Schiller, in his "Song to the Friends," which some of these friends may have related to the resurrection: "Everything repeats itself in life, eternally young is only the fancy, that which has never and nowhere happened, that alone does not grow old." In these lines, it is true, Jesus is accorded the mythical immortality of a Prometheus, or a Faust, or King Lear. However, he is at the same time removed from all historical reality. The Jewish man of God from Galilee is disembodied into a Greek figure of legends— in crass contradiction to the faith in divine revelations within the innerworldly life which characterizes the whole Bible.

(3) The third possibility would be that the reports of the resurrection rest on visions of individual persons who experienced them as real experiences but so that they are completely inaccessible to the objective test of the sciences. Most Jewish scholars consider this third possibility as the most likely one: It could have been a case of honest autosuggestion—as we find it now and then in the Talmud. Disciples see their departed master in a dream. A woman speaks with her deceased husband in a vision. A whole table fellowship believes strongly in the prophet Elijah, sees him present, and speaks with him. Where the power of faith is involved, Jews have a power of imagination that sometimes borders on the super-

natural—without any need to doubt the subjective honesty of that which is experienced.

In regard to the future resurrection of the dead, I am and remain a Pharisee. Concerning the resurrection of Jesus on Easter Sunday, I was for decades a Sadducee. I am no longer a Sadducee since the following deliberation has caused me to think this through anew. In none of the cases where rabbinic literature speaks of such visions did it result in an essential change in the life of the resuscitated or of those who had experienced the visions. Only the vision remains which was retold in believing wonderment and sometimes also embellished, but it did not have any noticeable consequences.

It is different with the disciples of Jesus on that Easter Sunday. Despite all the legendary embellishments, in the oldest records there remains a recognizable historical kernel which cannot simply be demythologized. When this scared, frightened band of the apostles which was just about to throw away everything in order to flee in despair to Galilee; when these peasants, shepherds, and fishermen, who betrayed and denied their master and then failed him miserably, suddenly could be changed overnight into a confident mission society, convinced of salvation and able to work with much more success after Easter than before Easter, then no vision or hallucination is sufficient to explain such a revolutionary transformation. For a sect or school or an order, perhaps a single vision would have been sufficient—but not for a world religion which was able to conquer the Occident thanks to the Easter faith. Professor Klausner said in Jerusalem in answer to the question whether Jesus had lived at all:

> If the four evangelists should have freely invented such believable and broadly agreeing reports about the Nazarene, then that would be a greater miracle than all the miraculous deeds of Jesus tied together.

Something similar is probably also true of the resurrection. If the defeated and depressed group of disciples overnight could change into a victorious movement of faith, based only on autosuggestion or self-deception— without a fundamental faith experience — then this would be a much greater miracle than the resurrection itself.

In a purely logical analysis, the resurrection of Jesus is "the lesser of two evils" for all those who seek a rational explanation of the worldwide consequences of that Easter faith. The true miracle is the fact that this Jewish group of Jesus' followers came to faith, a miracle which, like all miracles, escapes any exact description or scientific proof.

Any kind of deception is excluded in any case, be it the theft of the body, trance, or the invention of a miracle, for then—Joseph Klausner stresses this—"their subsequent belief (would be) utter trickery and fraud. That is impossible. *Deliberate imposture* is not the substance out of which the religion of millions of people is created" (*Jesus of Nazareth*, p. 357). It also says of John the Baptist, "a righteous and holy man," that he, after his martyr's death by Herod "has been raised from the dead"—and then his opponents asserted that his disciples had come, picked up his body, and buried it in a tomb (Mark 6:14-29).

This recalls not only the rumor that Jesus' "disciples came by night and stole him away" (Matt. 28:11ff.), but also the ascension of Elijah which even among the disciples of the prophet encountered wide disbelief: "They sent therefore fifty men; and for three days they sought him but did not find him. And they came back to (Elisha) . . . and he said to them, 'Did I not say to you, Do not go?' " (2 Kings 2:17f.).

Faith and doubt run like twin threads crosswise through the whole history of Israel. The manner in which the resurrection took place is today just as uncertain as it was in Hillel's time, when the controversy concerning the general resurrection of the dead occupied rabbis (Genesis Rabbah 14 and Leviticus Rabbah 14) but wisely was left open. In the word of the Jesuit Father F. Letzen-Deis: "At the present situation of research one can . . . not assert that the evangelists wanted to impose on us the supposition that the words and deeds of the Risen One took place exactly as it is printed there. . . . The whole *how* of the appearances remains closed to us" ("Auferstehungserfahrung und Osterglaube," *Theologische Akademie*, Vol. 7, Frankfurt a.M. 1970, p. 84 ff.).

Be that as it may, something must have happened which we can designate as a historical event since its

results were historical—although we are completely unable to comprehend the exact nature of the occurrence.

I remember an old folk song which I heard recently
in Berlin:

> At Easter in Jerusalem,
> Something happened.
> That is still wonderful today,
> Not everyone can comprehend it.

I can believe in such a real Something which in a purely rational way can neither be proved nor refuted—a
Something that does not rest on the wish as the father
of the thought, nor is it a mirage. I cannot believe in the
empty tomb nor in the angels in white garments nor in
the opening of the heaven nor in the absurd miraculousness of the so-called Gospel of Peter. All that belongs to
the pious fraud of later generations which themselves no
longer felt the direct impact—but tried to whip up enthusiasm by means of embellishing the truth. If one re-
moves cautiously all these literary additions, a certain
"something" remains for us which in the apostles' simple
manner of expression has been called resurrection.

Modern theologians frequently use strange paraphases
for the resurrection of Jesus:

• "Jesus has risen into the kerygma," says Rudolf Bultmann.

• "He has risen because he has conquered the innermost

center of all earthly being eternally in his death," says Karl Rahner.

- "The faith in the resurrection is an Old Christian form of expression . . . which we today cannot accept as obligatory for ourselves," writes Herbert Braun.

- "Easter means: The cause of Jesus goes on," declares Willi Marxsen for whom the resurrection is an "interpretament" of the early church, i.e., a way of interpreting an unexpected event.

- "The event which we designate according to late Jewish tradition with the metaphor 'resurrection from the dead' does not mean a change but a confirmation of Jesus." Thus Heinz Zahrnt.

- "To believe in the resurrection of Jesus means to undertake the surprising risk to reckon with Jesus Christ as a present reality," says Meinrad Limbeck.

All this may be true and correct. I don't know. But most of these and similar conceptions strike me as all too abstract and scholarly to explain the fact that the solid hillbillies from Galilee who, for the very real reason of the crucifixion of their master, were saddened to death, were changed within a short period of time into a jubilant community of believers. Such a post-Easter change, which was no less real than sudden and unexpected, certainly needed a concrete foundation which can by no means exclude the possibility of any physical resurrection.

One thing we may assume with certainty: neither the Twelve nor the early church believed in the ingenious wisdom of theologians! Indeed, they hardly would have understood what the gentlemen of scholarship want to say in such a roundabout manner.

I cannot rid myself of the impression that some modern Christian theologians are ashamed of the material facticity of the resurrection. Their varying attempts at dehistoricizing the Easter experience which give the lie to all four evangelists are simply not understandable to me in any other way. Indeed, the four authors of the Gospels definitely compete with one another in illustrating the tangible, substantial dimension of this resurrection explicitly. Often it seems as if renowned New Testament scholars in our days want to insert a kind of ideological or dogmatic curtain between the pre-Easter and the risen Jesus in order to protect the latter against any kind of contamination by earthly three-dimensionality. However, for the first Christians who thought, believed, and hoped in a Jewish manner, the immediate historicity was not only a part of that happening but the indispensable precondition for the recognition of its significance for salvation. For all these Christians who believe in the incarnation (something which I am unable to do) but have difficulty with the historically understood resurrection, the word of Jesus of the "blind guides, straining out a gnat and swallowing a camel" (Matt. 23:24) probably applies.

If God's power which was active in Elisha is great enough to resuscitate even a dead person who was thrown into the tomb of the prophet (2 Kings 13:20ff.), then the bodily resurrection of a crucified Jew also would not be inconceivable. "Or have I no power to deliver?" (Isa. 50:2), asks the Lord of those who are hard of believing.

A Messianic Midrash

"You seek Jesus the crucified?" Thus it says in the Gospel: "He is not here; for he has been raised from the dead." These words, at the empty tomb, were a completely Jewish answer, the spiritual home of which lies in the field of tension between prophecy and apocalyptic. Expiatory suffering, a martyr's death and resurrection belong to that Jewish doctrine of salvation which until today is expressed in the examples of the patriarch Isaac who sacrifices himself voluntarily, of Isaiah's suffering servant of the Lord, and of the death-defying valor of the Maccabean blood witnesses.

"Be gracious to your people, O God," says Eleazar the priest on the pagan torture rack. "Let the punishment be sufficient which we are suffering for their sake. Let my blood serve as a cleansing for them; as a substitute for their soul take my soul . . . after these words, the noble man died in the tortures," thus we read in the Fourth Book of Maccabees (6:28).

"And Abraham took the wood of the burnt offering." These words from Genesis 22:6ff. which speak of Abraham's willingness to sacrifice, and "not to spare his own son," are elaborated by the Midrash Rabbah: "As one who takes the cross on his shoulders."

"God . . . did not spare his own Son but gave him up for us all," thus writes Paul later (Rom. 8:31f.)—a reinterpretation which he probably "received in tradition" out of the mouths of the same original witnesses who told him about the resurrection (1 Cor. 15:3ff.).

The ethical enthusiasm, the messianic thirst for salvation, and the impatient longing for the kingdom of God, which brought men of God like Jesus to the point where they sought salvation for all of Israel in their own perishing, were no less Jewish.

Finally, the debate between the followers and opponents of Jesus concerning the significance of Golgotha was traditionally Jewish.

While suffering and the death on the cross were for the one side the last proof of failure and defeat, for the other side they became the sign of God's acceptance of the self-sacrifice of Jesus. The same events which brought the ones to despair filled the others with certainty of salvation.

Was the resurrection reported by the disciples a human *taking*-in-advance—or a divine *giving*-in-advance of life in the coming world? That was the controversy which divided Jews and Jewish Christians at that time in Israel. "You are the anointed one!" Peter says to Jesus (Mark 8:29). "This is the king Messiah!" Rabbi Akiba says to Bar-Kokbha a century later (Ta'anit 68b).

When, however, both failed as saviors of Israel, their numerous followers—depending on the strength of their faith—split: the undeterred called him "Bar Kokbha"— the son of the star—, according to the messianic interpretation of Numbers 24:17 ("A star shall come forth out of Jacob").

The disappointed called him "Bar Kosiba"—the son of the lie—in the bitterness of their defeat. The undiscouraged disciples on their way to Emmaus called Jesus "A prophet mighty in deed and word"—even after the crucifixion. But those in Israel (Baraitha to Sanhedrin 43a) who could not forgive him the breakdown of the messianic hopes they had pinned on him called him "A magician who has deceived Israel."

Basically, both schools were "prisoners of hope," as the prophet Zechariah (9:12) rightfully calls his incorrigible optimists of salvation. People who so often had experienced suffering and God's election as closely related could say already at the time of the Maccabees: "The Lord reproves him whom he loves" (Cf. Prov. 3:11f.). For many a pious Jew it was only a small step from this truth to the connection of messiahship and a martyr's death on the Roman cross. It was this conception that he "carried our sorrows" so that "with his stripes we are healed," that prepared the way for faith in the resurrection (Isa. 53:4, 5).

From a rabbinic point of view the resurrection is basically a messianic Midrash of the first community of Jesus which grew out of the confidence in God's loving righteousness and of the faith in Jesus as the proclaimer of salvation who was sent by God. It is not difficult to understand historically how this came about. That passover of death with the oppressive fact of the cross must have rested like a curse on the disciples of Jesus from the first day. Their believing survival depended on how they coped with this fact, for the search for meaning and the urge to interpret belong to the very soul of Judaism just as much as circumcision. They *had to* learn to understand the historical events as God's work as Israel has done since the Exodus—in order to master them constructively in an understandable and reflective way.

That which dawned upon them like a lightning flash of hope was then a new interpretation of the Scripture which combined Isaiah 53 and Ezekiel 37 in an illuminating way:

> The just consciously bears injustice which he encounters innocently in order to effect God's forgiveness and grace for his penitent followers by his vicarious suffering of expiation.

This was a new, comforting interpretation of the suffering servant of God in the light of the vision of the dead bones. And so they succeeded in illuminating their own experience of Jesus prophetically in such a way that now the sacrificial death, the expiation, and the redemption were fused together into a tremendous experience of God—an experience that helped them to interpret death as transition, the cross as a touchstone, and the resurrection as a down payment for life eternal.

Not as the redemption—for obvious reality contradicted this—but as a definite pledge of God, as a down payment of further hope for the longed-for complete redemption which we all are still expecting. In whatever way the first followers of Jesus may have understood their master—as a prophet, Messiah, or proclaimer of the beginning kingdom of God—they seem unanimous in retrospect in their experience of the resurrection of the crucified one as the "Yes for all the promises of God" (2 Cor. 1:20) which made it possible for them to endure faithfully until the "God of hope" (Rom. 15:13) would grant them the fulfillment. The disciples of Jesus stood solidly within their native Judaism to which belongs also the unequivocal faith in the resurrection.

Thus the Pentecost testimony of the apostles that this murdered Jesus had risen again (Act 2:23f.) was indeed for the Sadducees nothing but a painful stumbling block (Acts 4:1f.; 5:17ff.); but for the Pharisees, as for the majority of all Jews, it was a problem seriously to be investigated (Acts 5:34ff.; 23:6ff.), since for them the resurrection—also of individual dead persons—lay entirely in the realm of the possible (Sanhedrin 90b).

Jewish biblical scholars and rabbis of our time who are the spiritual heirs of those Pharisees have given expression to this opinion in various ways:

- Rabbi Samuel Hirsch wrote already in the year 1842:

  In order that Jesus' power of hope and greatness of soul should not end with his death, God has raised in the group of his disciples the idea that he rose from death and continues living. Indeed, He continues living in all those who want to be true Jews.

- Rabbi Leo Baeck saw in the faith in the resurrection an integral part of Jesus' Jewish environment and of the thought world of his followers. In the year 1938 he wrote concerning Jesus,

  Before us there stands a man who gained his disciples from among his own people. They were seeking the Messiah, the son of David, the promised one, and they found and beheld him in Jesus. His disciples in Israel believed in him even beyond his death so that it became to them an existential certainty that he—as the prophet foretold—had risen from the dead on the third day.

- Rabbi Samuel Sandmel sees in the faith in the resurrection a confirmation of the incomparableness of Jesus,

  Only a Jew whose unique combination of qualities was extraordinary could have been thought

by other Jews to have been accorded a special resurrection. (*A Jewish Understanding of the New
Testament*, Cincinnati, 1957, p. 28f.).

- J. Carmel, the Israeli teacher and author who regrets
  that the Gospels are not at home in the framework of
  Jewish literature, writes, "If the prophet Elijah has
  ridden in a fiery chariot into heaven, why should not
  Jesus rise and go to heaven?" (In reference to L.
  Baeck, S. Sandmel, and J. Carmel, see my book *Ist das
  nicht Josephs Sohn?*, München-Stuttgart, 1976).

- The philosopher of religion Samuel Bergmann wrote
  in regard to Martin Buber's book *Two Types of Faith*,
  "Not the living but the dead and risen Jesus is the
  founder of Christianity" (*Freiburger Rundbrief*
  XXVII, 1975, No. 101/104 p. 3). In one of his letters
  to Martin Buber, dated May 30, 1949, Bergmann
  wrote:

  I did not succeed in understanding the difference
  between the faith in Sinai and the faith of Paul
  as the "acceptance of the facticity of an event
  which does not flow out of concrete reality."
  What does "concrete" mean here? Why do the
  "legends" of miracles of resuscitation not belong
  here? They certainly did not appear as legends to
  the Jews of the time of Jesus. If the "hard real-
  ism" of the Jews in matters of the body can be
  broken through only on the basis of an eschatological total view, so it has to be said on the other

hand that the Messiah was expected for any hour
and that therefore the possibility of a resurrection
was very real in any and every hour. For instance
Rabbi Jeremiahu (Jerusalem Talmud, Kilayim
9:4) gives detailed instructions how he should be
buried in order that he would be ready when the
Messiah comes. If it were really the case that Jews
could not acquiesce in the resurrection of an individual, then the manner in which Peter's report
of the resurrection is received by the gathered
Jewish community in Acts 2 would be completely incomprehensible. Therefore the thesis seems
unfounded to me that in the Jewish world of
faith the fact that an individual rose from the
dead as an individual does not find room. After
all, it is not just any individual but the Messiah
(Ibid., p. 4.).

The Testimony
of Maimonides

Since the first century, the attempt has often been made to invalidate all supernatural elements of this Easter experience:

The disciples themselves stole the body of Jesus in order to invent the resurrection; "Juda the gardener" transferred him to another tomb; it was a coma; another was nailed to the cross in Jesus' place; or: it is simply a case of mass psychosis or of ecstatic hallucinations. All this has been known and rehashed ever since that first Easter.

On the "theft of the body," Joseph Klausner says that it is equally difficult to suppose that the disciples themselves would steal the body. During the first few days they were too terrified by the frightful death of their

Messiah "so that they would not have dared to move the body from the tomb" (*Jesus of Nazareth*, p. 357). In regard to all kinds of deception or malicious fraud, Klausner adds:

> Here again it is impossible to suppose that there was any conscious deception. . . . There can be no question but that some of the ardent Galileans saw their lord and Messiah in a vision. . . . This vision . . . was treated as faithful proof of the Resurrection of Jesus . . . it became the basis of Christianity (p. 359).

The question which can no longer be avoided is: Is it possible for deceivers or self-deceived to establish a faith that conquers half the world? In other words, can swindlers let themselves be tortured and persecuted in the name of an illusion—up to joyful martyrdom? Or is all this only a monumental error? Are there errors of a thousand years that are able to bring forth world-embracing institutions of faith?

If I were a convinced atheist, I could say yes to these questions without difficulty. The godless world of the atheists and agnostics is ruled by a blind happenstance that is unwilling to recognize either the plan of salvation or the providence of God.

It can hardly be determined today whether it was Peter who on his own overcame the tragedy and the absurdity of Golgotha and was able to understand the crucifixion as Jesus' victory over his conquerors and as a transition to the kingdom of God (as Machovec seeks to explain in his atheistic book about Jesus), or whether external circumstances let the gladdening recognition dawn on him that the martyr's death was not the last word from God.

Be that as it may, as a faithful Jew, I cannot explain a historical development which, despite many errors and much confusion, has carried the central message of Israel from Jerusalem into the world of the nations, as the result of blind happenstance, or human error, or a materialistic determinism—although all these factors possibly may have helped advance the divine plan of salvation. The experience of the resurrection as the foundation act of the church which has carried the faith in the God of Israel into the whole Western world must belong to God's plan of salvation.

Confirmation for this supposition comes from a high rabbinic authority:

> All these matters which refer to Jesus of Nazareth . . . only served to make the way free for the King Messiah and to prepare the whole world for the worship of God with a united heart, as it is written: "Yea, at that time I will change the speech of the peoples to a pure speech, that all of them may call on the name of the Lord and serve him with one accord" (Zeph. 3:9). In this way the messianic hope, the Torah, and the commandments have become a widespread heritage of faith —among the inhabitants of the far islands and

among many nations, uncircumcised in heart and flesh.

This is what Maimonides wrote in his monumental work *Mishneh Torah* (Hilkhot Melakhim XI, 4).

Other rabbinic authorities—e.g., Juda Halevi, Menahem Meiri, Leon Modena, Moses Rivkes, and Jakob Emden—saw in Christianity not only a valid way of salvation but also a *praeparatio messianica*, in agreement with Isaiah (42:6; 49:6), Jeremiah (4:2), and Zephaniah (3:9) which would result in the universal conversion of all people to God (compare "Rabbis Concerning Jesus," in my book: *Ist das nicht Josephs Sohn?* pp. 81-167).

If the global ecumenical prophecy of Zephaniah belongs to the central hope of Jews and Christians as it is affirmed by the Talmud, Martin Luther, and the Second Vatican Council, as well as by the liturgy of the synagogue, then the Christianizing of a billion people is a significant way station on the road toward the conversion of the world to God.

Since this Christianizing is based irrevocably on the resurrection of Jesus, the Easter faith has to be recognized as a part of divine providence. All these matters that refer to Jesus, Maimonides says, have to include his resurrection also, for without it "the messianic hope, the Torah, and the commandments" would never "have become a widespread heritage of faith."

Undoubtedly a mystery surrounds this resurrection, a mystery which makes all cunning pale into insignificance. "There are more things in heaven and earth, . . .

than are dreamt of in your philosophy." This word of
Hamlet applies especially to all honest theology whose
beginning and end lies in the humble knowledge of our
ignorance, and in the conviction that we never can
comprehend God.

Aside from this *docta ignorantia* of all theologians
which makes the indisposability of God and his way of
salvation a biblical commonplace, would it not be
unbiblical arrogance to suggest to unnumbered millions
of God-believing Christians that their faith rests on a
falsification, an error, a figment of the imagination of a
handful of Jews from Galilee?

As is well known, the church stands and falls with the
resurrection of Jesus from the dead. Already Paul asserts
that with unambiguous emphasis, and all the evangelists
follow him in this matter. No less clear is the fact that
everything the later Gentile church could gather about
this resurrection comes without exception from Jewish
sources, since all witnesses of the Risen One were Jews.

Therefore, if one wants to deny the genuineness of
this Easter experience or questions the faith in its genuineness, how can one avoid the implication that the
churches altogether are based on fraud or self-deception?
If a Jewish-Christian dialogue is to be honest, this basic
question cannot be avoided.

The resurrection of Jesus was ambiguous as an event,
but unambiguous in the history of its effect. For the fact
is incontrovertible that the world church which was
founded in the name of Jesus originated out of his death.

Where the life history of Jesus ends, the history of Christianity begins. But this is not enough.

The death of a martyr can indeed cause admiration and emulation, but it never has had a religious meaning in itself—least of all in Judaism which puts such a positive value on life and has never glorified suffering or death.

Only that which comes *after* this earthly death—his being made alive through God, his participation in the "coming world," his eternal life with God—illuminates this painful, apparently futile death with religious meaning. From reflection on this death, both Jews and Christians can gain a meaning for themselves from the death of their martyrs. He died as "a lamb without blemish," as "expiation for others," as a selfless sacrifice "for us"— this is often stated in the martyrologies of both religions, in concepts which originate in the Jewish realm of faith.

Basically, the resurrection was for the disciples an indication that their master had achieved through his death as a martyr what Jews had hoped for from their martyrs since the time of the Maccabees. In the words of what is perhaps the oldest Jewish-Christian interpretation of the cross: "For Christ *also* died for sins once for all, *a* righteous *one* for the unrighteous, that he might bring us to God, being put to death in the flesh but made alive in the spirit" (1 Peter 3:18). Here Jesus is called "a righteous one"—among others—who with so many Jews before and after him gave his life for God and his people.

If desertion by God and suffering mortal tortures are
the end of a great hope-filled person, how can people
continue to hope for goodness and justice amidst a world
that remains both inhumane and alienated from God?
Many in Israel who then knew of Golgotha were confronted with these questions—until the disciples' testimony of the resurrection revived many a ruined hope
and enabled them to cope with all the barbs of doubt.
Only the resurrection opened their eyes and hearts for
the paradox which lies at the roots of every faith. Death
was neither a defeat nor ruin but. . . . Here the interpretation differed although all of them sensed his cross
in retrospect as a consequence of his selfless ministry and
of his example of the righteous Kingdom of God.

"You shall be holy; for I the Lord your God am holy"
(Lev. 19:2). In the paraphrase of the Nazarene, "You,
therefore, must be perfect, as your heavenly Father is
perfect" (Matt. 5:48). He was concerned about the
imitation of God which should force or accelerate salvation—so that it could become a rule of behavior for
all believers in a world which was, and still is, out of
joint.

Indeed this world remains unsaved, and we all are still
suffering in it just as we also are still responsible for it.
But that experience of a handful of Bible-believing Jews
who were able to carry their faith in God into the Gentile
world must surely be interpreted as a God-willed encour-
agement in a world that so often seems hopeless.

Our Common Hope

What is certain in all this is the fact that the word of Jesus concerning the grain of wheat has become historical reality: "Unless a grain of wheat falls into the earth and dies, it remains alone; but if it dies, it bears much fruit" (John 12:24). In the words of Rabbi Hiyya, the son of Joseph: "When a grain of wheat which is buried at night rises with so many glorious garments, so and still even more will the righteous" (Ketubbot 111a).

Rabbi Pinhas of Koretz was asked, "Why should the Messiah be born on the anniversary of the destruction of the Temple—as the tradition has it?" Rabbi Pinhas answered, "The kernel, which is sown in earth, must fall to pieces so that the ear of grain may sprout from it. Strength cannot be resurrected until it has entered deepest secrecy" (M. Buber, *Tales of the Hasidim:*

The Early Masters, New York: Schocken, 1947, p. 123).

How many of such "kernels of wheat" were not carried to burial in Israel and died away—without bearing earthly fruit! It would seem that only this kernel of wheat fell into the fertile soil of faith so that his death helped innumerable people the world over to a better life and an immortal hope.

All honest theology is a theology of catastrophe, a theology that receives its impulse from the misery and the nobility of our human nature:

• from the fear of death, from the will to live, and from the great hope that not everything is at an end when death comes;

• a hope that arises from an anticipation of that incomprehensible infinity and final reality which we call God;

• a hope that cannot acquiesce in the thought that our existence begins with birth pangs and a whimper—only to end with a final rattle of agony;

• a hope that tears, death, and mourning will not have the last word;

• a hope that draws from its confidence "upward" the courage to look "ahead"; courage beyond dying to a life beyond the grave which deprives death of its sting in order to give our life a meaning which cannot perish or decay;

• a hope that grants the power to commit oneself without question to the God who "kills and makes alive"

(Deut. 32:39) and does not forget his righteous ones (Ps. 37:25).

That is the quintessence of the biblical faith in the resurrection, both of Jews and Christians.

If one could gain an insight into the soul of today's surviving remnant of Israel in order to discover its understanding of itself, one would most likely draw the conclusion that Auschwitz and the founding of the State of Israel stand in the same spiritual relationship with each other as Good Friday and Easter Sunday do in the heart of believing Christians. The same abyss yawns between cross and the resurrection as between the mass Golgotha of the Hitler years and the national resurrection in the year 1948.

Without the resurrection of Jesus, after Golgotha, there would not have been any Christianity—just as Auschwitz without the successive new foundation of Israel could have meant the end of the Jewish people. For what Christian can ever know how much unfounded confidence and faith in the future is needed in order to bring Jewish children into the world since 1945?

Thus the cause of Jesus is basically the cause of Israel. Both the doctrine and the suffering, the faith-experience of God, the survival after martyrdom, and the eternal life for which we hope. Here I see the uniqueness of the basic meaning of that salvation event on Passover-Easter Sunday in Jerusalem.

A resurrection of our hope for life which Jews and Christians affirm in common:

Thy dead shall live, their bodies shall rise. O dwellers in the dust, awake and sing for joy! For thy dew is a dew of light, and on the land of the shades thou wilt let it fall (or: the earth shall bring life to the dead. Isa. 26:19).

One last question: Must the resurrection of the dead be a miracle?

The works of our creator are altogether wonderful—but not miraculous. They do not arbitrarily skip the natural chain of cause and effect like the works of the sorcerer in the fairytale. There is, for example, the wonder of the human ovum. Nothing but matter can at first be determined. Twenty years later, a being has come into existence which has broken through the barriers of plant and animal life, can say "I," and is able, against the trend of its impulses, to love selflessly.

Seen in a larger framework, that means that at the beginning there was dead matter. Out of this matter arose life in a "development" that lasted for billions of years. Out of life, consciousness gradually arose, and out of consciousness, with great effort and over a long period of time, love and self-knowledge. This can be called a global or comprehensive resurrection from that which was dead. Such wonderful work indeed does not become less grandiose through the fact that we envision more and more intermediate steps of its "evolution." Is not every tree, every flower, and every child a wonder of God? But through the rust and verdigris of everyday life, we have become so hardened that we need a Shakes-peare, a Johann Sebastian Bach, and a van Gogh in order to learn astonishment anew.

Why should the resurrection of a personal ego after passing through death be more miraculous than the grad-ual awakening of a human being out of the lifeless mat-ter of a fertilized ovum? And if the physicists affirm that in this inexhaustibly large universe not a single ounce of substance is lost but just changes its form, why should the most precious gift that God wanted to give us, a spark from his fire, the breath from his spirit, dis-appear without a trace after our earthly decease? To argue otherwise would not only give the lie to all confi-dence of salvation but would also contradict the ele-mentary logic of natural science. Thus the hope of resur-rection is a reasonable faith which should be sufficient for a meaningful, fulfilling life on earth.

EPILOGUE

Jesus, therefore, without doubt, belongs to the *praeparatio messianica* of the full salvation which is still in the future. He was a "paver of the way for the King Messiah," as Maimonides calls him, but this does not mean that his resurrection makes him the Messiah of Israel for Jewish people. In the words of the Catholic theologian Clemens Thoma:

> For Jewish scholars, the testimony of the resurrection was no proof for the messiahship of Jesus because for them the concept of resurrection is not connected with the messianic expectation of salvation. At the time of Jesus, Judaism was expecting the resurrection of various figures: of Enoch, of Moses, of Elijah, of Jeremiah, . . . but not the resurrection of the Messiah. . . .

> Through the resurrection of Jesus, an access to
> faith in the *one*, until then unknown, God of Is-
> rael was opened to the Gentiles.
>
> On the other hand, in Judaism the faith of God
> did not need to receive new foundations and rea-
> sons; it was unquestioned. . . . For Israel, God was
> on earth already before Christ" (*Kirche aus Ju-
> den und Heiden*, p. 45).

I therefore can accept neither the messiahship of Jesus
for the people of Israel nor the Pauline interpretation
of the resurrection of Jesus. I am not striving for any
kind of syncretism between Judaism and Christianity.
On the other hand, a dialogue between Jews and Christians can be carried on seriously only if the Jewish part-
ner also starts out with the assumption that Christianity
is a faith fellowship desired by God which concerns him
"for God's sake," even if he does not see in it a way
which he himself can or must go. Two ways of faith
such as Judaism and Christianity, which have a common
origin and hope for a common messianic goal, should
devote their dialogue not only to the polite contact at
the edges and to the removal of the tensions of the past,
but should seek contact from center to center. Without
glossing over or bypassing the differences, a dialogue in
which both partners take the faith substance of the other
as seriously as their own could become a true dialogue—
from open faith to open faith, from confidence to confi-

dence, from emphatic searching and finding, and from joy in the duality which knows its ultimate unity only in God. This book is dedicated to that concern.

GLOSSARY

The definitions of the terms used in this book are based on the *Encyclopedia Judaica*.

ABOTH—Ethical treatise of the Mishnah, known as Pirke Aboth, "Sayings of the Fathers."

AGGADAH—Name given to those sections of Talmud and Midrash containing homiletic expositions of the Bible, stories, legends, folklore, anecdotes, and maxims. In contradiction to *halakah*.

B.C.E.—Before the Common Era; equivalent to B.C. in Christian reckoning.

BARAITHA—Statement of a rabbinic teacher not found in the Mishnah.

BERAKHOTH—Tractate in Mishnah and Talmud dealing with benedictions.

C.E.—Common Era; equivalent to A.D. in Christian reckoning.

HAGGADAH—Ritual recited in the home on Passover eve at seder table.

HAGIGAH—Tractate of Mishnah and Talmud dealing with peace offerings during festivals (Deut. 16:16-17).

HALAKAH—Those parts of Talmud concerned with legal matters.

HALLEL—Term referring to Psalms 113-118 in liturgical use.

HASIDIM—Here it refers to the religious movement founded by Israel Baal Shem Tov in the first half of the 18th century that emphasized pietism and mysticism.

HILLEL—Most prominent Jewish teacher from about 30 B.C.E.-10 C.E. Famous for both his scholarship and his saintliness.

KADDISH—Liturgical doxology.

KETUBBOT—Tractate of Mishnah and Talmud dealing with marriage contracts.

KIDDUSH—Prayer of sanctification recited over wine or bread on the eve of Sabbaths and festivals.

KILAYIM—Tractate of Mishnah and Talmud dealing with various laws (Deut. 22:9-11).

MEGILLAH—Tractate of the Mishnah and Talmud dealing with Purim.

MEKHILTA—A collection of rabbinic teachings on Exodus.

MIDRASH—A method of interpreting Scripture to elucidate legal points *(Midrash Halakhah)* or to bring out lessons by stories or homiletics *(Midrash Aggadah)*. Also name for a collection of such rabbinic interpretations.

MISHNAH—The earliest codification of Jewish Oral Law (completed c. 200 C.E.). Its tractates are discussed and commented on in the Talmud.

PESACH—Passover.

PESAHIM—Tractate in Mishnah and Talmud dealing with Passover.

PURIM—Festival commemorating the delivery of the Jews of Persia at the time of Esther.

RABBAH—An exegetical Midrash which gives a consecutive exposition of a biblical book, chapter by chapter, verse by verse, and often even word for word. There is a Rabbah on each of the five books of the Pentateuch as well as Ruth, Song of Songs, Lamentations, Ecclesiastes, and Esther.

RABBAN—Honorific title, higher than that of rabbi, applied to heads of the Sanhedrin in mishnaic times.

ROSH HA-SHANAH—Here, a tractate of Mishnah and Talmud dealing with new years.

SANHEDRIN—Here, a tractate of Mishnah and Talmud dealing with Judges. Also, the assembly of ordained scholars which functioned both as a supreme court and as a legislature before 70 C.E.

SEDER—Ceremony observed in the Jewish home on the

first night of Passover (outside Israel, the first two nights), when the Haggadah is recited.

SHAMMAI (c. 50 B.C.E.-c. 30 C.E.)—One of the leaders of the Sanhedrin. Founded a great school that generally represented the conservative opinion compared with the lenient views of the school of Hillel.

TA'ANIT—Tractate of Mishnah and Talmud dealing with fast days.

TALMUD—"Teaching"; a compendium of discussions on the Mishnah by generations of scholars and jurists in many academies over a period of several centuries. The Jerusalem (or Palestinian) Talmud mainly contains the discussions of the Palestinian sages. The Babylonian Talmud incorporates the parallel discussions in the Babylonian academies. Lower case j (or p) or b before the tractate reference indicates which Talmud is being quoted.

TARGUM—Aramaic translation of the Bible.

TORAH—The Pentateuch or the Pentateuchal scroll for reading in the synagogue. Also, the entire body of traditional Jewish teaching and literature.

YALKUT SHIMONI—The best known and most comprehensive midrashic anthology covering the entire Hebrew Bible.

YEVAMOT—Tractate in Mishnah and Talmud dealing with Levirate marriage (Deut. 25:5-10).

BIBLIOGRAPHY

H. Braun, *Jesus of Nazareth*, Philadelphia: Fortress, 1979

M. Buber, *Tales of the Hasidim: The Early Masters*, New York: Schocken, 1947

H. Danby, *The Mishnah*, Oxford: Clarendon, 1933

Freiburger Rundbrief, Beiträge zur christlich-jüdischen Begegnung, Schriftleitung: Dr. Gertrud Luckner, Freiburg i. Br.

Haggadah of Passover, tr. M. Samuel, New York: Hebrew Publishing Co., 1942

J. Hertz, *The Authorized Daily Prayer Book*, New York: Bloch, 1971

J. Jeremias, *New Testament Theology: The Proclamation of Jesus*, New York: Scribner's, 1971

J. Klausner, *Jesus of Nazareth*, New York: Macmillan, 1953

H. Küng, *On Being a Christian*, Garden City: Double-day, 1976

P. Lapide, *Ist das nicht Josephs Sohn?*, Stuttgart/München, 1976

F. Lentzen-Deis, "Auferstehungserfahrung und Oster-glaube" in *Theologische Akademie*, vol. VII, Ed. K. Rahner and O. Semmelroth, Frankfurt a. M., 1970

G. E. Lessing, *Eine Duplik* (1778), Lessings Werke, Leipzig

W. Marxsen, *Die Sache Jesu geht weiter*, Gütersloh, 1976

S. Sandmel, *A Jewish Understanding of the New Testament*, Cincinnati, 1957

A. Schweitzer, *The Quest of the Historical Jesus*, New York: Macmillan, 1961

E. Schweizer, *Jesus*, Richmond: John Knox, 1971

C. Thoma, *Kirche aus Juden und Heiden*, Biblische Informationen über das Verhältnis der Kirche zum Judentum, Wien, 1970